THE
DEVELOPMENT OF
CHESS STYLE

BY

DR. M. EUWE

*Translated
from the Dutch
by*
W. H. COZENS

DAVID McKAY COMPANY, INC.
NEW YORK

Originally published in 1966 in The Hague as
Veldheersschap op de Vierenzestig

First paperback edition, 1978

ISBN: 0-679-14045-X

LIBRARY OF CONGRESS CATALOG CARD NUMBER: 78-51942

10-9-8-7-6-5-4-3-2-1

MANUFACTURED IN THE UNITED STATES OF AMERICA

PREFACE

THE LAST part of my book *Praktische Schaaklessen* contained a certain amount of chess history. This, with a little revision and a great deal of amplification, forms the basis of the present work. In particular, games and characteristic features of the play of the most outstanding masters of the last fifty years have been added.

The aim of this book is *not* to make any contribution to the dissemination of historical chess knowledge; the author hopes rather that by analysing the ideas of successive periods and by tracing the development of different schools of thought the reader's outlook may be broadened and his appreciation of the strategic and tactical problems of chess deepened.

DR. M. EUWE

Amsterdam, 1966

CONTENTS

INTRODUCTION

CHAPTER 1. Excursions with the pieces (Greco, 1600?–1634?)   1
  Game 1. About 1625   2
  Game 2. Analysis dating from about 1625   4

CHAPTER 2. The Discovery of the Pawns (Philidor, 1726–1795)   6
  Game 3. From Philidor's writings   7

CHAPTER 3. Long Live Combination! (Anderssen, 1818–1879)   11
  Game 4. Anderssen–Kieseritzky   12
  Game 5. Anderssen–Dufresne   14
  Game 6. Anderssen–Zukertort   16
  Game 7. Anderssen–Zukertort   19

CHAPTER 4. Combination for Strategic Ends (Morphy, 1837–1884)   22
  Game 8. Schulten–Morphy   23
  Game 9. Morphy–Stanley   26
  Game 10. Morphy–Allies   28
  Game 11. Bird–Morphy   29
  Game 12. Morphy–Harrwitz   32

CHAPTER 5. Positional Play (Steinitz, 1836–1900)   36
  A. His Career   36
  B. His Teachings   38
  C. Elucidation of his Teachings   39
    (1) Lead in Development   40
    (2) Superior Mobility   40
    (3) Occupation of the Centre   42
    (4) Unsafe King-position   42
    (5) Weak Squares   43
    (6) The Pawn Position   47
      (*a*) United Pawns   48
      (*b*) Isolated Pawns   48
      (*c*) Doubled Pawns   49
    (7) The Q-side Majority   50
    (8) Open Files   52

(9) The Advantage of the Two Bishops 53
(10) Material Preponderance 54
(11) Conversion of Temporary Advantages into Permanent
    Ones 54
D. Games played by Steinitz 56
Game 13. Steinitz–Mongredien 56
Game 14. Steinitz–Chigorin 58
Game 15. Zukertort–Steinitz 61
Game 16. Janowsky–Steinitz 66
Game 17. Steinitz–Fleissig 69
Game 18. Zukertort–Steinitz 71
Game 19. Pillsbury–Steinitz 74
Game 20. Lasker–Steinitz 77
Game 21. Neumann–Steinitz 82

CHAPTER 6. Technique and Routine (The Virtuosi, 1900–1914) 90
Game 22. Tarrasch–Steinitz 91
Game 23. Lasker–Napier 95
Game 24. Pillsbury–Lasker 98
Game 25. Lewitzky–Marshall 101
Game 26. Maróczy–Marshall 103
Game 27. Rotlewi–Rubinstein 107
Game 28. Capablanca–Marshall 109
Game 29. Schlechter–Teichmann 112
Game 30. Capablanca–Duras 112

CHAPTER 7. The Independent Thinkers (Between the Wars:
    1919–1940) 114
Game 31. Allies–Capablanca and Réti 117
Game 32. Réti–Gruber 119
Game 33. Réti–Alekhine 122
Game 34. Sämisch–Nimzovitch 125
Game 35. Bogolyubov–Alekhine 127
Game 36. Flohr–Johner 129
Game 37. Fine–Alekhine 131
Game 38. Euwe–Reshevsky 133
Game 39. Keres–Walther 135

CHAPTER 8. New Thirst for Battle (The Russian School: 1945
    to the Present Day) 139
Game 40. Lyublinsky–Botvinnik 140
Game 41. Smyslov–Reshevsky 143
Game 42. Tal–Larsen 145
Game 43. Petrosyan–Kozali 147
Game 44. Keres–Spassky 150

INTRODUCTION

To SUPPOSE that the history of any subject should be just a collection of independent facts is a serious misapprehension. They may, it is true, make interesting reading; but they may also have little significance for the subject in question.

The history of chess—under its present rules—is the study of the growth and gradual change of the strategic ideas of leading players of succeeding generations. Taking note of this evolution and thoroughly grasping it is the very thing which makes for better judgment and an increase in playing strength. The development of a chess player runs parallel with that of chess itself; a study of the history of playing methods therefore has great practical value.

Chess has certainly existed for twelve hundred years, but during the earlier part of this time its rules were different from ours. Only during and after the Renaissance did it assume its present form. The first phase of its development dates from about the beginning of the 16th century when the modern game took shape. The beginning of its ever-growing literature belongs to the same period.

Succeeding generations of experts have contributed to the development of chess play, but mostly it was the style of some outstanding individual which moulded the thinking and style of play of his time. It is with the most famous of these trail-blazers that this book concerns itself.

In the various chapters the chess player may perhaps be able to trace the evolution of his own play; he may be able to check which milestones of growth are already behind him, and see how many more remain to be passed before he reaches the final stage. How far he will get in the end one cannot say; but it is safe to state that each player has to start by grappling with somewhat naïve problems in the style of the 16th and 17th centuries. This is no more to be avoided than is the opening phase of a game.

EXCURSIONS WITH THE PIECES
Greco (1600?–1634?)

THE FIRST stage of growth is the most difficult and lasts the longest: so it was in the story of chess.

The primitive chessplayer lived, so to speak, from hand to mouth. He made his move and hoped for the best. It was a matter of excursions with the pieces, punctuated by pleasant little episodes such as winning a piece or giving check—especially giving check, which had a rare fascination for the early players. But systematic play was virtually non-existent; what happened on the board was largely a matter of chance.

Progress first manifested itself in the extent to which players were able to profit from more or less fortuitous opportunities; and in this respect the most typical figure from the early days of chess was Greco.

The following two games are taken from the manuscript written by Greco about 1625. The author evidently possessed an incisive power of combination and ability to see clearly into complicated situations. His manuscript consists largely of a collection of pretty tactical devices—to which, however, the best defences were often not taken into consideration. They show one player going all out for mate while the other plays to win as much material as possible. These are chess fairy-tales on the age-old theme of the conflict between riches and honour; and very attractive fairy-tales they are, albeit somewhat primitive to present-day sensibilities.

The Calabrese, Gioachino Greco, was born about 1600 and died not later than 1634. He was the first great genius in the story of modern chess. His life was short, but the examples which he worked out set the pattern for a hundred years; some live on to the present day as an integral part of chess theory.

Adroit utilization of a fortuitous opportunity. The style of the 17th century.

About 1625.   *King's Gambit*

| 1. P—K4 | P—K4 |
| 2. P—KB4 | P—KB4 |

A weak move. Perhaps they liked the look of this quadrangle of pawns in the centre.

3. KP × P

With the troublesome threat of 4. Q—R5 ch. This check can hardly be prevented, for 3. .... Kt—KB3 fails against 4. P × P.

| 3. .... | Q—R5 ch |

The Queen has to move to make way for the King. She could have gone to K2 direct, but Black takes his opportunity to give the first check. Check to the King! This always affords satisfaction to the beginner, even though in sober fact it may have no significance at all.

| 4. P—Kt3 | Q—K2 |
| 5. Q—R5 ch | |

This check is decidedly weak. The indicated line was 5. P × P, Q × P ch; 6. B—K2! by which means White could at least have secured an important lead in development on account of the premature movements of the black Queen. On the other hand, in this variation (5. P × P, Q × P ch) the interposition 6. Q—K2 would be wrong, allowing Black to regain the gambit pawn by 6. .... P—Q3; e.g. 7. Q × Q ch, P × Q; 8. B—Kt2, Kt—QB3; 9. P—KKt4, P—KR4; 10. P—KR3, Kt—B3; etc.

| 5. .... | K—Q1 |
| 6. P × P | |

Just about forced, in view of Black's threat of 6. .... P × P ch. However, the black Queen now comes into better play.

| 6. .... | Q × P ch |
| 7. B—K2 | |

After this, White can neither hold the gambit pawn nor yet give it back advantageously. Nor could he have achieved this latter object by 7. Q—K2, for after 7. .... Q × BP the white QB-pawn is en prise, and if White then continues 8. P—Q4 there follows 8. .... Kt—KB3 with a troublesome threat of 9. .... B—Kt5 ch followed by 10. .... R—K1.

| 7. .... | Kt—KB3 |
| 8. Q—B3 | P—Q4 |

Attacking the KB-pawn.

9. P—KKt4

This attempt to hold the B-pawn is futile, and leads only to a weakening of the white King's position. It would have been better to relinquish the pawn at once by 9. P—Q4, meeting either 9. .... Q × QP or 9. .... Q × BP with 10. B—Q3.

| 9. .... | P—KR4! |

The first strong move in this game. Black sees that the white KKt-pawn must move, whereupon the KB-pawn loses its protection and will be lost.

10. P—KR3?

And this is the first tactical blunder. Up to now, though the moves had been naïve, in the manner of beginners, neither player had made any definite oversight. It was essential to play 10. P—Kt5. Then after 10. .... Kt—K1 the KB-pawn would have been lost, but White would still not have been in any real trouble.

10.	P × P
11. P × P	R × R
12. Q × R	Q—Kt6 ch?

Dazzled by the chance of a check Black neglects his best continuation, which was simply 12. .... Kt × P. This would have led at least to the win of the KB-pawn as well, leaving Black with a strong extra pawn and a good position.

13. K—Q1?

Overestimating the power of a check and paralysed by the fear of it, as the novice at the chess-board still is today. The King looks safest at Q1, but in fact 13. K—B1, protecting the Knight, would have been much more to the point. Then after 13. .... Kt × P; 14. Q × P ch, B—Q2; 15. B × Kt, Q × B; 16. Kt—QB3 the game would still have been about even.

| 13. .... | Kt × P |

Now this capture leads at least to the same advantage as Black could have obtained by force by 12. .... Kt × P.

14. Q × P ch?

A move to shout about. White wins a pawn and gives check into the bargain!

Actually it is only this move which allows Black to achieve his aim, for the KKt is now entirely without protection, so

that White is no longer able to take off the dangerous black Knight. The only defence was 14. B × Kt, which, after 14. ...., Q × B ch; 15. Kt—K2, Q × P would have conceded only a pawn.

| 14. .... | B—Q2 |

After this simple covering move White is defenceless. The trouble is that 15. B × Kt loses a piece by 15. ...., Q × Kt ch; 16. K—K2, Q × B ch.

15. Kt—KB3

Whereupon Black forces mate with a manœuvre which is both neat and—for that period—certainly very original.

15.	Kt—B7 ch
16. K—K1	Kt—Q6 ch
17. K—Q1	Q—K8 ch
18. Kt × Q	Kt—B7
	mate.

1

Smothered mate!

The diagram shows convincingly that in those days players had little use for systematic development. Look at the white Q-side pieces!

The pretty finish does show, however, that when an opportunity presented itself they knew how to play a neat combination.

GAME 2

Greco was really ahead of his time in the matter of style. Here is a specimen of his treatment of the opening known in England nowadays as the Giuoco Piano and in most other countries as the Italian Game. An Analysis dating from about 1625. Giuoco Piano

1. P—K4	P—K4
2. Kt—KB3	Kt—QB3
3. B—B4	B—B4
4. P—B3	Kt—B3
5. P—Q4	P × P
6. P × P	B—Kt5 ch
7. Kt—B3	

This is regarded today as the main line of the Giuoco Piano. The pawn sacrifice implicit in the text move was for a long time considered incorrect, but about the end of the 19th century, Greco's continuation was rehabilitated.

7.	Kt × KP
8. 0—0	Kt × Kt

8. ...., B × Kt at this point was long held to be the refutation of Greco's pawn sacrifice. The continuation 9. P × B, P—Q4! is indeed in Black's favour, and this was the only line considered. The stronger move 9. P—Q5!, however, introduced by Möller, gives White an attack which guarantees at least a draw.

On the other hand, the text move (8. .... Kt × Kt) used to be very much underrated. Not until about three hundred years after the appearance of Greco's manuscript was it demonstrated—by Dr. Bernstein—that Black can get a reasonable game in this way.

9. P × Kt	B × P

Current opinion is that 9. .... P—Q4 is also playable here without any serious disadvantage.

9. .... B—K2, however, is less good, White obtaining an overwhelming attack with 10. P—Q5.

10. Q—Kt3	B × R

This is where Black completely misses the mark. The text move loses, and 10. .... B × QP, which was also examined by Greco, is no better. But Black has a good continuation—namely, 10. .... P—Q4!; 11. B × P, 0—0!, etc., with about even chances. This is the defence put forward by Bernstein in the 1930s.

11. B × P ch	K—B1
12. B—Kt5	Kt—K2
13. Kt—K5!	

2

An extraordinarily fine attacking move. White intends 14. B—Kt6, threatening mate on KB7; with the text move he also vacates KB3 for his Queen.

Less convincing, though also good enough for White, is the line 13. R—K1, P—Q4; 14. B × Kt ch, Q × B; 15. R × Q, K × R; 16. B × P. Black has a material equivalent for his Queen, but his King is badly misplaced.

14.	B—Kt6!	P—Q4
15.	Q—B3 ch	B—B4
16.	B × B	B × Kt
17.	B—K6 ch	B—B3
18.	B × B	K—K1

Black's only hope.

13. ....   B × P

If, say, 13. .... P—Q3, White's 14. B—Kt6 is just as decisive.

19. B × KtP

And White wins. The double threat of 20. Q—B7 mate and 20. B × R wins a piece for White, and his attack continues unabated.

This line of the Giuoco Piano is known as the Greco Variation. It is to be found in all standard works on chess theory and stands as a worthy memorial to the great Calabrese.

THE DISCOVERY OF THE PAWNS
Philidor (1726–1795)

RIGHT UP to the 18th century the pawn was considered a negligible quantity. Chess theory, in this respect, had reached the stage of the present-day novice. Pawns were useful only for purposes of promotion—that is to say, in the endgame.

It was Philidor who first realized and demonstrated the great importance of the pawns in the opening and middlegame. 'The pawn is the soul of the game' he declared; and this statement is still accepted nowadays as not in the least exaggerated.

Since the whole career of a pawn is limited to five or six irreversible moves every pawn advance requires to be weighed up most carefully; and since, moreover, the pawn position is of decisive importance for the active placing of the pieces, the security of the pawns themselves is of paramount importance. They must therefore be set up economically—preferably in a tight phalanx.

These and other facts concerning the pawn position, such as the disadvantages of isolated, scattered, backward and doubled pawns, were first discovered and enunciated by Philidor. It was he also who first realized the significance of the good and bad Bishop, though he held the incorrect opinion that from a purely defensive point of view the bad Bishop could render better service than the good.

For the planning of the game Philidor gave several important rules —for instance these two:

'It is always advantageous to exchange the KB-pawn for the adverse K-pawn, for in this way one gains control of the centre and at the same time places the KB-file at the disposal of the Rooks.'

'It is frequently dangerous to attack too soon; one should not start an attack until the pawns which have to sustain it are properly supported. Without this precaution the attack will be quite useless.'

François André Danican-Philidor was born on the 7th September, 1726, in Dreux. He came from a musical family and was himself a professional musician. He must have felt the call of chess quite early for he was only 22 when he produced his famous book *L'Analyse des Echecs.* He wrote it in Holland, where he stayed repeatedly in the course of his roving life. *L'Analyse* was published in London in 1749. There was a second edition in 1777 and a third in 1790. It consisted of nine copiously annotated games together with some valuable end-game investigations. By illustrating his principles in this book the author laid the first stone in the edifice of modern position play. He took chess out of the narrow confines of Euclidean observation into the boundless realm of Cartesian thought.

Philidor died on the 25th August, 1795—a misunderstood and disappointed man. His pawn theory was still not fully grasped at that time, particularly by his immediate successors. The trouble was that Philidor himself was not altogether happy in the application of his theories. He tended to go too far, deeming the pieces hardly more than the servants of the pawns, and underestimating their powers. For instance, after 1. P—K4, P—K4 he considered the advance of the KB-pawn so important that he condemned 2. Kt—KB3 because of the reply 2. .... P—Q3 and 3. .... P—KB4, recommending instead 2. B—B4 (not, however, the immediate 2. P—KB4, for such a squandering of a pawn was not in his line at all). This and other similarly exaggerated conclusions, as well as his fantastic tales of the history of chess, damaged Philidor's reputation. A full century had to elapse before the pawn-lore of the great Frenchman was reinstated by Steinitz and refined to its true worth.

GAME 3

Elucidating the pawn theory of Philidor.
A game from Philidor's writings. Bishop's Opening.

1. P—K4
'The King's Pawn moves two steps' says Philidor. Here we have the earliest form of the descriptive notation which is still used in England and a few other places.

1.	P—K4
2. B—B4	P—QB3
3. P—Q4	

'It is absolutely essential to push this pawn two squares to obstruct the enemy game; if he could push his Q-pawn two squares and attack your Bishop he would seize the advantage of the move.'

Philidor is here pointing out that White must not content himself with 3. P—Q3 because Black would reply 3. .... P—Q4, occupying the centre and thus appropriating the advantages of the first move. This observation—and for that matter almost the whole of his annotation—is absolutely correct, even in the light of the latest knowledge.

3. .... P × P
'If, instead of taking your pawn, he had moved his Queen's pawn two squares an entirely different game would have arisen,

giving rise to our first divergence.'

By 'first divergence' he means what we should call 'first variation'. Under this heading Philidor examines the consequences of 3. .... P—Q4 and shows that White gets the advantage.

| 4. Q × P | P—Q3 |
| 5. P—B4 | B—K3 |

'There are two reasons for this move:

1. To enforce P—Q4 and thus free the K-Bishop.
2. To exchange the white K-Bishop which is a latent threat to the KB-pawn.'

| 6. B—Q3 | P—Q4 |
| 7. P—K5 | |

This is in accordance with Philidor's theories. White establishes a pawn majority on the K-side and lays the foundation for a later breakthrough. For the time being the game takes on a more-or-less closed character.

| 7. .... | P—QB4 |
| 8. Q—B2 | Kt—QB3 |

'If, instead of completing his development, Black had gone on pushing pawns he would have been in danger of losing the game. It must be observed that pawns pushed too far forward can easily get lost, unless all the pieces are in play to support them. Two pawns abreast on the fourth rank are usually stronger than two on the sixth rank.'

This last statement evidently refers to the particular case when the pawns on the sixth rank are difficult to defend.

| 9. P—B3 | P—KKt3 |

There is a much stronger move in 9. .... P—B3! for 10. P—B5? is refuted by 10. ....Kt × P. Philidor often fails to take such tactical points into consideration and so is not successful in making out a convincing case for the great importance of his theories.

| 10. P—KR3 | P—KR4 |

'To prevent White's P—KKt4. It is to be observed that at the moment the two sides are equal in pawns, White having 4-3 on the K-side, and Black having 4-3 on the Q-side. Whoever first succeeds in breaking up the pawns in the sector where his opponent is strongest will probably win the game.'

Philidor is here discussing the struggle against a pawn majority and he deems it a great success to break up the oncoming phalanx. In this his judgment is quite correct, and this is why the above-mentioned move 9. .... P—KB3 would have been more in line with Philidor's own theory.

| 11. P—KKt3! | |

'This move is essential, for Black was threatening to separate the white pawns by P—R5. The KKt-pawn would then have been unable to link up with the KB-pawn without running the risk of being taken by the black R-pawn.'

This comment is absolutely valid, even in the light of modern ideas.

11.	Kt—R3
12. Kt—B3	B—K2
13. P—QR4	

The beginning of operations against Black's Q-side majority.

Compare the note to 10. ....
P—KR4.

13. ....   Kt—B4
14. K—B1

A move characteristic of Philidor's style. In itself the move is meaningless, for the King stands no better on B1 than on K1, but White is luring his opponent on.

14. ....   P—R5

Apparently very strong; but this is the very move which White's previous move was intended to provoke.

15. P—KKt4

Relatively the best move. White would rather concede the Exchange than have his pawn chain broken. Philidor reckons the advance P—KKt4 worth more than the Exchange.

15. ....   Kt—Kt6 ch
16. K—Kt2   Kt × R
17. K × Kt

3

'Although White is the Exchange down his position is probably superior. Notwithstanding the material loss the white King is quite safe, and White will be able to start an attack no matter which side Black may castle.'
Thus Philidor.

The position is certainly difficult, but the conclusion that White has the advantage perhaps goes rather far. It is noteworthy, incidentally, that the Russian chess school (see Chapter 8) also holds original views on the value of the Exchange.

17. ....   Q—Q2
18. Q—Kt1

'It is necessary to protect KKt4 lest Black should sacrifice his Bishop for two pawns, as he doubtless intended. For since the strength of White's position rests in his pawns it would be to Black's advantage to destroy them. The attack would then pass into Black's hands.'

18. ....   P—R4

A weak move. The proper way to make use of the extra material would be to open some lines. Black should have played 18. .... P—Q5!, especially as the attempt to keep the position closed by 19. P—B4 could be favourably answered by 19. .... Kt—Kt5.

19. B—K3

Tempting Black to play P—B5, which would suit White very well, enabling his Knights to infiltrate right into the Black game via Q4 and QKt5.

19. ....   P—Kt3

Even now Black should still have played P—Q5. A possible sequel: 20. P × P, B—Q4; 21. QKt—Q2, P × P; 22. B × QP?, Kt × B; 23. Q × Kt, B × Kt ch; 24. Kt × B, Q × Q; 25. Kt × Q, 0—0—0! with advantage to Black.

20. Kt—R3   0—0—0
'Black castles on the Q-side in order to escape the power of the white K-side pawns, which are further advanced than those on the Q-side.'

Even now the advance P—Q5 was still to be considered.

21. B—R6 ch   K—B2
22. Kt—B2
'22. Kt—Kt5 ch on the other hand would have endangered the Bishop and resulted in the loss of several moves.'

22. ....   R—R1
23. B—Kt5   Q—Q1
'In order to play Q—KB1, reinforcing the QB-pawn against which White can build up a rapid attack.'

24. P—Kt4

4

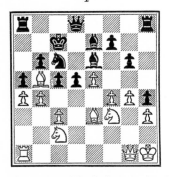

Now that Black has seriously weakened his K-position by his last two pawn moves, White himself proceeds to open up the lines.

24. ....   Q—KB1
Logical, but weak. Over and over again the same contrast is noticeable with Philidor—fine strategy with inferior tactics.

Both by 24. .... RP × P; 25. P × P, P—Q5, and by 24. .... P—Q5 direct, Black could still have obtained good chances.

25. P × BP   P × P
26. Kt—Q2
'To continue the attack on QB5 by means of Kt—Kt3.'

26. ....   P—B5
Preventing Kt—Kt3.

27. Kt—B3
White is now in full possession of his Q4 and has thus achieved decisive positional advantage. The breakthrough must result in an attack which in the present circumstances will play itself.

White's advantage depends almost exclusively on the pawn position and has been built up by systematic operations. In principle it matters little that it has been achieved partly by unsound means.

27. ....   P—B3
This hastens the end.

28. B—Kt6 ch   K—Kt2
29. B × Kt ch   K × B
30. Kt(3)—Q4 ch K—Q2
If 30. .... K × B there follows 31. Kt × B ch, B—B4; 32. Q—Kt1 ch, winning the Queen.

31. P—B5
The white phalanx in action.

31. ....   B—Kt1
32. P—K6 ch   K—K1
33. Kt—Kt5   B—Q3
34. Q—Q4
With the deadly and unanswerable threat of 35. Q × QP. White wins.

LONG LIVE COMBINATION!
Anderssen (1818–1879)

PHILIDOR INFLUENCED the style of his immediate successors in a totally unexpected way. The fact that the examples with which he sought to substantiate his pawn theories were on the whole not very convincing (see Game 3), resulted in the true value of his teachings being overlooked. Players were only spurred on to do better by tactical means.

After the period of the peasants—the pawns—there came the Napoleonic reaction. The hegemony of the pieces came to the fore again, if possible even more strongly than before. The quiet, rather unattractive, position play of Philidor lost its appeal; incisive attacks and combinations were the order of the day.

The spirit of Greco reawakened, and under more favourable conditions. With two centuries of experience and compilation behind them, players now had a good idea of the possibilities latent in the initial set-up, and they knew a lot about the openings. They looked for attacking positions with combinative possibilities, and they knew how to achieve such positions. In the course of time, moreover, they had acquired considerable proficiency in the attacking use of the pieces; and so, under full sail, and blown indirectly by the breeze of Philidor, they drove ahead across the wonderful seas of combination.

Material, and pawns in particular, counted for little. Gambits were played by choice and other openings were treated in similar style. Everything turned on attack and counterattack. Passive play, defence, refusal of sacrifices, the giving of one's attention to such 'miserable' objectives as the setting up of a pawn phalanx—these and all such ideas were right outside the mentality of the chessplayer of the first half of the 19th century. He was spellbound by the beauty of combination, and in this realm indeed many an elegant production was the result. The most brilliant protagonist of this style was Adolf Anderssen, a mathematics teacher from Breslau, born 6th July, 1818, died 9th (or some say 13th) March, 1879.

Anderssen scored the triumph of his life at the London Tournament of 1851. This was the first international chess tournament ever held. The best players of many lands were gathered together, and after about a month's play Anderssen won handsomely. Of his other successes the most notable was the winning of the Baden-Baden International Tournament of 1870.

In 1858 Anderssen had to yield the position of strongest player in the world to Morphy—only temporarily however for Morphy soon withdrew from chess completely. Anderssen remained at the summit of the chess Olympus until 1866, when he was beaten in a match by Steinitz by the not very convincing score of 8–6. Right to the end he remained one of the best and most active players of his time. In the history of chess Anderssen goes down as the most enthusiastic, the purest and, all things considered, the most ingenious combinative player of all time.

He represents, however, not the starting point of new methods but rather the highpoint of the old. He was no pedagogue. His concern was not for sober truth. In his chess he sought only for beauty. And how shall beauty be analysed and confined within rules?

The following fine wins are characteristic of Anderssen and also of the style of the period.

GAME 4

This is the so-called Immortal Game—a plain demonstration of Anderssen's disdain for material.

WHITE: A. ANDERSSEN   BLACK: L. KIESERITZKY
London, 1851. (Not from the tournament.)   *Bishop's Gambit*

1. P—K4	P—K4
2. P—KB4	P × P
3. B—B4	Q—R5 ch

The Classical Defence to the Bishop's Gambit. Today 3 .... Kt—KB3 is considered best for Black.

4. K—B1   P—QKt4
This is good in principle: Black offers a pawn to expedite his development. He fears that otherwise the insecure position of his own Queen may be more serious than the fact that White has forfeited the right to castle.

4. .... P—Q4, however, was preferable.

5. B × KtP	Kt—KB3
6. Kt—KB3	Q—R3

The Queen would have been much better off at R4.

7. P—Q3   Kt—R4
Thus the B-pawn is doubly protected and there is a threat of Kt—Kt6 ch. Apparently Black had relied too much on this move when playing 6. .... Q—R3.

8. Kt—R4	Q—Kt4
9. Kt—B5	P—QB3

Intending to follow up with 10. .... P—Q4 with nice counterplay.

10. P—KKt4
Leading to a fine piece sacrifice.

10. ....   Kt—B3
Now both the Bishop and the KKt-pawn are attacked.

11. R—Kt1!
The point. The black Queen will now be driven into a tight corner and White will get an enormous lead in development.

11.	**P × B**
12. P—KR4	**Q—Kt3**
13. P—R5	**Q—Kt4**
14. Q—B3	

With the primary threat of 15. B × P, winning the Queen. White already dominates the game.

14. ....   Kt—Kt1
This makes matters worse. It was essential for Black to try to break the enemy attack by the counter-sacrifice 14. .... Kt × KtP.

15. B × P   Q—B3
White's advantage in development would also have been decisive after 15. .... Q—Q1; 16. Kt—B3. It is typical that even in these circumstances Black still seeks to attack, and makes no attempt to bring his Queen into safety.

16. Kt—B3   B—B4
It makes no difference now what Black plays; White's attack is bound to prove irresistible.

17. Kt—Q5
Long live combination! Long live beauty in chess! White has an extraordinarily brilliant finish in view, and has no use for the simple, safe, winning move 17. P—Q4, pointed out by Réti. Regarded objectively the text move is less strong.

17. ....   Q × P
18. B—Q6
The sequel to White's previous move. Anderssen proceeds to offer both Rooks!

18. ....   Q × R ch
19. K—K2   B × R
Kieseritzky rises to the bait and is disposed of in immortal style. If 19. .... Q × R it would have been mate in two by 20. Kt × P ch, K—Q1; 21. B—B7 mate; or if 19. .... B × B, mate in four by 20. Kt × B ch, K—Q1; 21. Kt × P ch, K—K1; 22. Kt—Q6 ch, K—Q1; 23. Q—B8 mate.

But there was 19. .... Q—Kt7!, after which the issue would still have been uncertain.

20. P—K5!!

5

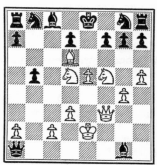

A problem move to crown the opus. With the black Queen away on QR8 shut off from the defence of KKt2 there is a main threat of 21. Kt × P ch, K—Q1; 22. B—B7 mate; and to this there is no satisfactory defence.

best in the circumstances; but after 21. Kt—B7 ch, K—Q1; 22. Kt × B! threatening both 23. B—B7 ch and 23.. Q × R the result would have been no more than a brief stay of execution.

20.	Kt—QR3

Now the mate follows in even prettier form. Most commentators give 20. .... B—R3 as

21. Kt × P ch	K—Q1
22. Q—B6 ch!	Kt × Q
23. B—K7 mate.	

GAME 5

Next to the 'Immortal' this is Anderssen's most celebrated game. Once again the decision is brought about by an extraordinarily deep and beautiful combination.

WHITE: A. ANDERSSEN   BLACK: J. DUFRESNE
Berlin 1852.   *Evans Gambit.*

1. P—K4	P—K4
2. Kt—KB3	Kt—QB3
3. B—B4	B—B4
4. P—QKt4	

The Evans Gambit, a very familiar opening at the time. White sacrifices a pawn so as to occupy the centre with gain of tempo.

4.	B × P
5. P—B3	B—R4
6. P—Q4	P × P

Today's verdict is that 6. .... P—Q3 is the best move here.

7. 0—0
A second pawn-sacrifice in the interests of rapid development.

7.	P—Q6

This is played in order to prevent White from achieving his desired centre formation by 8. P × P. For 7. .... P × P see Game 7.

8. Q—Kt3	Q—B3
9. P—K5	Q—Kt3

10. R—K1	KKt—K2
11. B—R3	P—QKt4

Black also plays for attack, but it looks risky to defer castling so long.

12. Q × P	R—QKt1
13. Q—R4	B—Kt3

After 13. .... 0—0? White would win a piece by 14. B × Kt.

14. QKt—Q2	B—Kt2
15. Kt—K4	Q—B4
16. B × P	Q—R4
17. Kt—B6 ch	

A powerful pseudo-sacrifice with the object of opening the K-file and putting an end to castling once for all.

17.	P × Kt
18. P × P	R—Kt1

Indirectly attacking the Knight. Presumably Black went into this line voluntarily in view of the open file which it gives him.

19. QR—Q1

The start of a sparkling combination. Various analysts have said that it would have been stronger to play 19. B—K4, threatening 20. B × Kt. But Anderssen had a very different attitude to chess. His decisions were guided by his powers of combination and his predilection for it.

6

19. ....   Q × Kt

Black accepts the offer and sets off a fine display of fireworks. All the critics agree that Black should have chosen 19. .... R—Kt5, as pointed out by Lipke in the *Deutsche Schachzeitung* in 1898, and that he would then have had good chances of saving the game. We shall presently show, however, that even after the text-move it remains an open question whether White has a forced win.

20. R × Kt ch   Kt × R?

After this White forces the mate in spectacular style. From the following analysis of the alternatives it appears that Black has at his disposal a line of play of which the consequences are still not clear:

A. 20. .... K—B1?; 21. R—K3 ch and White wins.

B. 20. .... K—Q1!; 21. R × P ch!

(1) 21. .... K—K1?; 22. R—K7 ch and White wins.

(2) 21. .... K × R?; 22. B—KB5 ch, K—K1; 23. B—Q7 ch; K—Q1; 24. B × Kt ch, and mate in a few moves.

(3) 21. .... K—B1!; 22. R—Q8 ch!

(*a*) 22. .... R × R? 23. P × Q, and White wins.

(*b*) 22. .... Kt × R?; 23. Q—Q7 ch!! K × Q; 24. B—KB5 ch and 25. B—Q7 mate.

(*c*) 22. .... K × R!; Best. Now there can follow:

(i) 23. B—K2 ch. According to most books this wins, but Black can continue 23. .... Kt—Q5! leaving White with no satisfactory continuation, let alone a forced win.

(ii) 23. B—Kt6 ch, Q × R ch; 24. Q × Q ch, Kt—Q5! with obscure complications.

(iii) 23. B—KB5 ch, Q × R ch; 24. Q × Q ch, Kt—Q5; 25. B—R3.

According to Collijn's *Lärobok* this is the winning line, but after 25. .... B—Q4 the outcome of this variation also remains doubtful.

21. Q × P ch!!   K × Q
22. B—B5 ch   K—K1
Or 22. .... K—B3, 23. B—Q7 mate.

23. B—Q7 ch   K—B1
24. B × Kt mate.

It is noteworthy that in both these celebrated games Anderssen gives mate with a Bishop on K7.

GAME 6

Here we see Anderssen holding on to his attack under difficult circumstances. In the nick of time another beautiful combination puts an end to the game.

White: A. ANDERSSEN　Black: J. H. ZUKERTORT
Barmen, 1869. *Evans Gambit*

1. P—K4	P—K4
2. Kt—KB3	Kt—QB3
3. B—B4	B—B4
4. P—QKt4	B × KtP
5. P—B3	B—R4
6. P—Q4	P × P
7. 0—0	B—Kt3

For 7. .... P—Q6 see Game 5.

| 8. P × P | P—Q3 |

The normal position in the Evans Gambit. White's central pawn-majority gives him nice attacking chances.

9. P—Q5

At the time this was considered the strongest move, but 9. Kt—B3 (see Game 9) is more in the spirit of the opening. After the text move the game quickly takes on a more-or-less closed character.

9.	Kt—R4
10. B—Kt2	Kt—K2
11. B—Q3	0—0
12. Kt—B3	Kt—Kt3
13. Kt—K2	P—QB4

Very properly Black seeks to swing the centre of gravity of the struggle over to the Q-side.

| 14. Q—Q2 | P—B3 |

Now White is made aware of the less attractive aspect of 9. P—Q5. His white-square Bishop has little scope, and it is difficult to open any lines on the K-side. Anderssen, however, has the knack of holding on to the attack.

| 15. K—R1 | B—B2 |
| 16. QR—B1 | |

The significance of this move will appear in due course.

| 16. .... | R—Kt1 |
| 17. Kt—Kt3 | P—Kt4 |

Little by little the situation is becoming critical. Black's Q-side majority is fully mobilized and his extra pawn is making itself felt. However, White's attack is also gaining strength.

| 18. Kt—B5 | P—Kt5 |

After 18. .... B × Kt; 19. P × B, Kt—K4; the value of White's 16. QR—B1 would be revealed by 20. Kt × Kt; for Black would have to reply 20. .... BP × Kt (20. .... QP × Kt?; 21. R × P) and then 21. P—B4 would be very strong.

The advance 18. .... P—B5 would have the disadvantage of making White's Q4 available for his Knights. After the text move, however, there is a strong threat of 19. .... P—B5 for after the forced 20. B × QBP Black would win the Exchange by 20. .... Kt × B; 21. R × Kt, B—R3. White's next move parries this threat.

| 19. R—KKt1 | B—Kt3 |

Now that the QB-pawn has an extra protection Black threatens 20. .... B×Kt; 21. P×B, Kt—K4; 22. Kt×Kt, QP×Kt with a good game.

20. P—Kt4	Kt—K4

20. .... B×Kt would not have the desired result now that White could reply 21. KtP×B.

21. B×Kt
There is no better service for this Bishop to render.

21.	QP×B?

Up to now attack and defence have kept pace with each other, but the text move is inferior since it allows White to open the KKt-file. 21. .... BP×B was the move.

22. R—Kt3	R—B2
23. P—Kt5!	

The combinative and decisive phase of the battle begins. White opens lines for his K-side attack.

23.	B×Kt
24. P×B	Q×P

There is no longer any satisfactory continuation.

7

The trenchant text move leads to a quick loss, but at least has the practical advantage of putting most difficulties in White's way.

25. P×P!
Thus White steers clear of two tempting continuations which would have turned to his disadvantage:

A. 25. B—B4?, Q×Q; 26. B×R ch, K×B; 27. Kt×Q, R—Q1; and Black has full compensation for the lost Exchange.

B. 25. P—Kt6? The idea is that after any move of the black Rook White wins the Queen by 26. B—B4. But after 25. .... R—Q2! the combination does not work, and it is Black who is better off.

25.	R—Q1

Not 25. .... R×P because of 26. B—B4, winning the Queen. But after the text move it looks as though Black is bound to come out on top because of his pin of the white Bishop.

26. R(1)—KKt1!
A hammer-blow. The threat is 27. R×P ch with mate in a few moves.

26.	K—R1

Inviting White to play 27. P×P ch (which he does!) and thus artificially close the KKt-file. White cannot capture at Kt7 with the Rook because of 27. .... Q×Kt ch. If Black had played 26. .... Q×B instead of the text move White would have won with 27. R×P ch as follows:

A. 27. .... K—B1; 28. R—Kt8 mate.

B. 27. .... K—R1; 28. Q × Q, R × Q; 29. R—Kt8 mate.

C. 27. .... R × R; 28. R × R ch:
(1) 28. .... K—B1; now White mates or wins the Queen, either by 29. R—Kt8 ch! or by 29. R—B7 ch!
(2) 28. .... K—R1; White can finish the game either by 29. R—Kt8 ch! etc., or by 29. Q × Q, R × Q; 30. Kt × P, etc., (or 30. Kt—Kt5, etc.).

27. P × P ch   K—Kt1
The hope that the King will be able to shelter safely behind the white pawn is doomed to disappointment. However, 27. .... R × P is just as useless; e.g.

A. 28. R × R, Q × Kt ch; 29. R(1)—Kt2. This is the simplest win. The continuation might be:
(1) 29. .... R × B; 30. R—Kt8 mate.
(2) 29. .... Q × B; 30. Q × Q, R × Q; 31. R—Kt8 mate.
(3) 29. .... P—K5; 30. R—Kt8 ch!, R × R; 31. Q—Kt2 ch with mate to follow.
(4) 29. .... P—B5; 30. Q—K1 (threatening 31. R—Kt8 ch), B—Q5; 31. B—K4, Q—R4; 32. Q—KKt1, Q—K1; 33. P—B6, etc.

B. 28. Q—R6. This is the most effective winning method. The main line runs 28. .... R(1)—KKt1; 29. B—K4! and now:
(1) 29. .... Q × B; 30. Q ×

P ch! K × Q; 31. R—R3 ch, Q—R5; 32. R × Q mate.
(2) 29. .... Q—B2; 30. Kt × P, Q—B1; 31. R × R, R × R; 32. R × R, Q × R; 33. Kt—Kt6 ch, K—Kt1; 34. B—Q5 ch, Q—B2; 35. Q—B8 mate.

28. Q—R6
White now threatens 29. Q × P ch, K × Q; 30. R—R3 ch, K—Kt1; 31. R—R8 mate; and against this there is nothing to be done.

28. ....   Q—Q3
Here Anderssen announced mate in five:

29. Q × P ch!
29. P—B6 would be less good because of 29. .... Q × B, protecting KR2.
Even so White would still win, by 30. Kt—Kt5, etc.

29. ....   K × Q
30. P—B6 ch!
After 30. R—R3 ch, Q—R3; 31. P—B6 ch, K—Kt1; (31. .... R × B; 32. P—Kt8(Q) mate), 32. R × Q, Black could still delay the mate by 32. .... R × BP.

30. ....   K—Kt1
Or 30. .... Q × B; 31. R—R3 ch, and 32. R—R8 mate.

31. B—R7 ch!   K × B
32. R—R3 ch   K—Kt1
33. R—R8 mate.
The masterpiece is complete!

GAME 7

In Anderssen's time careful defence was a thing unknown. The leading masters sought to meet every action with a counter-action, and never willingly played for mere consolidation. The following game is very characteristic in this respect.

White: A. ANDERSSEN   Black: J. H. ZUKERTORT
Berlin, 1871.   *Evans Gambit*

1.	P—K4	P—K4		
2.	Kt—KB3	Kt—QB3		
3.	B—B4	B—B4		
4.	P—QKt4	B × KtP		
5.	P—B3	B—R4		
6.	P—Q4	P × P		
7.	0—0	P × P		

The so-called Compromised Defence to the Evans—a risky line of play, for the acceptance of a second gambit pawn accentuates White's lead in development.

8.	Q—Kt3	Q—B3
9.	P—K5!	Q—Kt3

Not 9. .... Kt × P because of 10. R—K1, P—Q3; 11. Kt × Kt, P × Kt; 12. Q—Kt5 ch winning the Bishop.

10.	Kt × P	KKt—K2
11.	Kt—K2	P—Kt4

This counter-sacrifice—a sort of black Evans—was quite customary at the time (compare Games 4 and 5). Black returns one of his extra pawns in the interests of quick development.

12. B—Q3
But Anderssen prefers to keep up the attack.

12.	....	Q—K3
13.	Q—Kt2	

This threatens 14. Kt—B4, which would put the black Queen in real trouble.

13.	....	Kt—Kt3
14.	Kt—B4	Q—K2

14. .... Kt × Kt would have been simpler and better.

15. P—K6
An important exchanging transaction which definitely rules out K-side castling for Black. (Compare 17. Kt—B6 ch in Game 5).

15. ....   Kt × Kt
Other moves are inferior; e.g.:

A. 15. .... BP × P?; 16. B × Kt ch, P × B; 17. Kt × KtP and White wins.

B. 15. .... 0—0?; 16. P × P ch, Q × P; 17. Kt—Kt5, with a winning attack for White.

C. 15. .... QP × P; 16. Q × KKtP and Black will also be unable to castle Q-side.

16. Q × KKtP   R—B1
16. .... Kt × B? is refuted by 17. Q × R ch, Q—B1; 18. P × BP ch, K × P; 19. Q × P ch, and 20. Q × Kt.

17.	B × Kt	BP × P
18.	Q—Kt4	B—Kt2
19.	B × KtP	

This pawn is now captured, for after Black's Q-side castling the absence of the QKt-pawn will be a weakening of the King's position.

19. ....   0—0—0

From now on it will be blow for blow. Both sides have their open files and in this position Black's extra pawn will not play any great part. The first essential is well-placed pieces.

20. KR—B1

20. B—Kt5 achieves nothing: 20. .... Q—Kt2!

20. ....   R—Kt1
21. Q—R5

Threatening to win a piece by 22. B × Kt.

21. ....   B—B6

A move which thoroughly typifies the spirit of the age. Black reckons on 22. R × B, Q—Kt2, with the double threat of 23. .... Q × P mate and 23. .... Q × R. But White avoids the pitfall, and the Bishop on B6 remains badly placed. After the consolidating move 21. .... B—Kt3 the chances in this double-edged game would have been about even.

22. QR—Kt1   Q—B3
23. B—Kt3   B—Q5

Now Black has to lose time getting the Bishop to a better square.

24. B—R6!

8

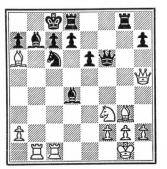

A brilliant combination. True, it leads to no direct advantage, but by eliminating the strong Bishop on Kt2 it renders Black's task more difficult. But for the time-consuming tour of the black Bishop R4—B6—Q5 this manœuvre would not have been possible.

24. ....   B—Kt3

Best. If 24. .... B × B there follows 25. Q—QR5!! threatening both 26. Q × B mate and 26. Q × P mate, and planning to meet 25. Kt × Q with 26. R × P mate. Black would then have to play 25. .... B—Kt3, after which by 26. Q × B ch, K—Kt1; 27. P—QR4 White would get an irresistible attack.

25. Q—QKt5   R × B?

Again typical of the style of the time—always fighting for the initiative. There was no thought of prudent defence; the constant aim was to begin a counter-attack at the earliest possible moment.

Black destroys White's dangerous Bishop on KKt3 and tastes the pleasure of calling the tune for the next two (!) moves. The right way was 25. .... Q—B4 with a tenable game; e.g.; 26. R—B5, Q × R(8) ch; 27. Q × Q, B × B, etc.

26. RP × R   Kt—Q5
27. Q—Q3

After 27. Kt × Kt, Q × Kt; 28. R—B2, Q—K5 White would have to exchange on QKt7, bringing his attack to a standstill.

27. ....   Kt × Kt ch
28. P × Kt   B × B
29. Q × B ch   K—Kt1
30. Q—B4

Threatening 31. Q × BP ch.

30.	K—R1
31. K—Kt2	R—KB1
32. R—Kt3	P—KR4
33. P—R4!	

Another combination, less spectacular but even deeper. It is far from obvious that with this advance of his QR-pawn White is preparing a decisive weakening of—QB6!

33.	P—R5
34. P—R5!	P—R6 ch
35. K—R1	

So as not to be exposed to further checks.

35.	B × RP

35. .... B × BP is decisively answered by 36. Q × BP.

36. Q—K4 ch!	P—Q4

36. .... P—B3 will not do because of 37. R × P! This is the first point of White's combination.

37. Q—QR4	

The second and real point: White brings his Queen with gain of tempo to the now unprotected square QB6. The black K-position will be blown to smithereens.

37.	B—Kt3
38. Q—B6 ch	K—Kt1
39. Q × BP ch	K—R1
40. Q—B6 ch	K—Kt1
41. R × B ch	P × R
42. Q × KtP ch	K—R1
43. Q—R6 ch	K—Kt1
44. R—Kt1 ch	Resigns

A game played by Anderssen with power and imagination far beyond the ordinary.

☆ 4 ☆

COMBINATION FOR STRATEGIC ENDS
Morphy (1837–1884)

THE ANDERSSEN era was interrupted by an apparition of dazzling brilliance.

There had already been rumours in Europe about the great successes which a certain Morphy had been achieving in America; but such news struck no great chill in the continent of Anderssen. It was unthinkable that Staunton, one of Europe's great ones, should accept the challenge to play a match in America against this stripling, Morphy.

But then Morphy made his appearance in England, and in no time at all European chess was dumbfounded. The 21-year-old American demolished prominent masters one after another in match-play. Morphy then proceeded to Paris where eventually he got his chance of meeting Anderssen—and even he had to admit defeat. By the impressive margin of 7–2 the German colossus was overthrown.

All this happened in the short time from the end of June to the end of December, 1858. Morphy remained in England for a few months, mostly giving blindfold séances, as a rule on eight boards. He created a sensation by the enormous strength which he displayed in this sort of play as well. But soon it was all over; after a five months interval the Anderssen era resumed its progress. Upon his return home in May, 1859, Morphy gave up serious chess, and from about 1864 he never touched the chessmen again. Some psychological defect had checkmated the greatest chess phenomenon of all time.

Paul Charles Morphy was born in New Orleans on the 22nd of June, 1837, and died in the same city on the 10th (or 11th) of July, 1884, his love for chess having changed, by degrees, into a deep revulsion. Morphy has left us nothing but his games—silent, sparkling testimony to his powers. These games excel in splendid attacks and combinations. Their fascinating style remains to this day the peak of perfection and inspiration. 'Morphy-like' has become an established adjective which means more to the chessplayer than 'perfect' and 'brilliant' combined.

Where then is the difference between Morphy and Anderssen? The latter was also a fully-equipped master of attack and combination. The form of the question suggests the answer: Morphy was all this and more. He was an accomplished position-player as well. His superiority lay in the building up of his game, in his attention to, and correct appraisal of, the general characteristics of a position. He was Anderssen's master in achieving the kind of position in which the sleeping beauty Combination needed only to be awakened; yet at the same time he felt at home in the type of position which did not lend itself to direct attack or combination.

Development, the centre, open lines; these, according to Steinitz, were the three leading principles which Morphy followed. They were for him prime objectives, absolutely fundamental factors in the battle, whereas for Anderssen they had real significance only insofar as they furthered some previously selected aim.

As a position-player Morphy was the disciple of Philidor and the forerunner of Steinitz; yet he won his games mostly in the manner of Anderssen, since his talent for combination was much greater than that of either of the two chess pedagogues just mentioned. His talent came into its own all the more easily on account of the fact that most of his opponents saddled themselves with some weakness or other right from the opening stage. This is the reason why Morphy is generally recognized only as a combinative player, whereas in fact, his most important victory—that against Anderssen—was due entirely to his better grasp of the general requirements of the position.

Here are a few typical Morphy games. Naturally they are for the most part fine achievements in the field of combinative play.

GAME 8

An illustration of Morphy's struggle for the initiative. An attack down the open file.

White: J. W. SCHULTEN   Black: P. MORPHY

New York, 1857. *Falkbeer Counter-Gambit*

| 1. P—K4 | P—K4 |
| 2. P—KB4 | P—Q4 |

This counter-gambit, originated by Falkbeer, was still new and little known. Black offers a pawn in order to take the initiative himself instead of ceding it to White by 2. .... P × P. Such tactics, pro-

vided too much risk was not involved, were right in Morphy's line.

Up to recently there were masters who considered the Falkbeer to be virtually a refutation of the King's Gambit. The latest research, however, gives White the better chances.

3. P × QP   P—K5

The black K-pawn now exerts strong pressure on White's position.

4. Kt—QB3

Up to about 1920 this move was reckoned inferior—perhaps on account of the present game; 4. P—Q3 was considered best. It now seems, however, that the text move also gives good chances.

4. ....   Kt—KB3
5. P—Q3

But this cannot be recommended. The right line is 5. Q—K2!, B—Q3; 6. P—Q3!, 0—0; 7. P × P, Kt × Kt; 8. Kt × Kt, R—K1; 9. Q—B3, P—KB4; 10. B—K3! and White holds the extra pawn without much difficulty.

5. ....   B—QKt5
6. B—Q2

Now Black is compelled to show his colours. Must he exchange on Q6 and then on QB6 as well in order to regain his pawn? This would give White the better game in all variations.

6. ....   P—K6!

Morphy to the finger-tips! This second pawn sacrifice retards White's development considerably and enables Black to mount a dangerous attack by rapid occupation of the open K-file.

7. B × P   0—0

Already the open K-file is playing its part, for Black threatens R—K1 with decisive advantage.

8. B—Q2

Best. White avoids the pin of this Bishop and unpins the Knight.

8. ....   B × Kt

All in the interests of the open file. This Knight might otherwise have blocked it at K2 or K4.

9. P × B   R—K1 ch
10. B—K2   B—Kt5

White now experiences great difficulty with his development.

11. P—B4

If 11. K—B1 or 11. P—KR3 there follows 11. .... B × B and 12. .... Kt × P, giving Black a powerful attack at the cost of only one pawn. White therefore tries to hold both extra pawns so as to have some substantial compensation for his unavoidable positional inferiority. But this policy makes his task still harder.

11. ....   P—B3!
12. P × P?

Consequent but deleterious. It was urgently necessary to relieve the pin on the K-file. White should have played either 12. P—KR3 or 12. K—B1.

12. ....   Kt × P

Now the threat is 13. .... Kt—Q5, decisively reinforcing the attack against K7. Against this White has no satisfactory defence.

13. K—B1

Too late, but other moves were even worse, e.g.

A. 13. K—B2. This would have received the same reply as the text move.

B. 13. P—KR3, B × B; 14. Kt ×
B, Kt—Q5 and Black wins a
piece.

C. 13. B—QB3, Kt—Q5; 14. B ×
Kt, Q × B;

  (1) 15. K—B1, B × B ch;
      16. Kt × B, R × Kt!; 17. K ×
      R, R—K1 ch.

    (*a*) 18. K—Q2, Kt—K5 ch
       and mate next move.

    (*b*) 18. K—B1, Kt—Kt5!
       and wins, for after
       19. Q × Kt White would
       lose both Rooks.

  (2) 15.   P—KR3,   B × B;
      16. Kt × B, R × Kt ch!;
      17. K × R, R—K1 ch;
      18. K—B1, Kt—R4! and
      wins.

  (3) 15. R—Kt1, R × B ch;
      16. Kt × R, R—K1 and
      wins.

  (4) 15.   Kt—B3,   B × Kt;
      16.   P × B,   Kt—R4;
      17.   R—KB1,   Kt × P;
      18. R—B2, R—K2 and
      there is no answer to the
      threat of 19. QR—K1.

13. ....   R × B

(*See diagram 9*)

This wins two pieces for a
Rook, with no slackening of the
attack.

14. Kt × R   Kt—Q5
15. Q—Kt1
Other moves are no better.

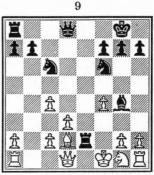

9

Position after Black's 13th move

15. ....   B × Kt ch
16. K—B2
If 16. K—Kt1, Black wins by
16. .... Kt × P with the main
threat of 17. .... Q—Q5 ch;
and 16. K—K1 is equally hopeless for White (16. .... Q—K2).

16. ....   Kt—Kt5 ch
17. K—Kt1
If 17. K—Kt3, Kt—B4 ch and
mate next move.

If 17. K—K1, Q—R5 ch;
18. P—Kt3, R—K1! and the
threat of 19. .... Kt—B6 mate
is deadly. After the text move
it is mate in seven.

17. ....   Kt—B6 ch
18. P × Kt   Q—Q5 ch
19. K—Kt2   Q—B7 ch
20. K—R3   Q × BP ch
21. K—R4   Kt—R3
22. Q—Kt1   Kt—B4 ch
23. K—Kt5   Q—R4
                      mate.

GAME 9

Illustrating Morphy's ideas on the Centre. The fundamental advantage of a mobile formation. Compare this with Game 6.

White: P. MORPHY   Black: C. H. STANLEY
New York, 1857. *Evans Gambit*

1. P—K4	P—K4
2. Kt—KB3	Kt—QB3
3. B—B4	B—B4
4. P—QKt4	B × P
5. P—B3	B—R4
6. P—Q4	P × P
7. 0—0	P—Q3
8. P × P	B—Kt3
9. Kt—B3	

A very remarkable move at that time. The usual line was 9. P—Q5 or else 9. B—Kt2 with the threat of P—Q5. It was deemed necessary to work all the time with threats.

But the advance P—Q5 always gives a closed character to the game, and later on White finds difficulty in keeping the attack going. This was pointed out in Game 6. Morphy generally attached more importance to maintaining the tension than to making immediate threats; in the present case he strives to maintain as long as possible the mobile front with pawns at K4 and Q4.

The text move achieves no instant advantage: it is played on principle. It is simply the result of general strategic ideas, and it was not until after Anderssen's time that their significance slowly percolated to all the leading players.

9. ....   Kt—B3
One of those tactical blunders which push the strategic element in Morphy's games into the background and steer the play at once into combinative channels. Just like Alekhine in the days when he was facing weaker opponents Morphy jumps at the opportunity to wield his mighty combinative powers. After 9. .... B—Kt5 (best met by 10. B—QKt5) or 9. .... Kt—R4 (which would be followed by 10. B—KKt5, P—KB3; 11. B—B4, Kt × B; 12. Q—R4 ch, Q—Q2; 13. Q × Kt, Q—B2; 14. Kt—Q5) White would have had more difficulty in justifying his central strategy.

10. P—K5!

10

This forces the opening of lines of attack against the black King.

10. ....   P × P
Practically forced, the attacked Knight having no decent move.

11. B—R3
The most important point of White's previous move: Black cannot castle.

11. .... B × P

If 11. .... P × P, White wins
by 12. R—K1 ch; e.g. 12. ....
B—K3; 13. Q—Kt3, Kt—QR4;
14. B × B!, Kt × Q; 15. B—B5 ch,
etc.

12. Q—Kt3

Threatening 13. B × P ch, K—
Q2; 14. Q—K6 mate.

12. ....   B—K3

A pawn is offered to stem the
white attack—but without success. If 12. .... Q—Q2 the
simplest continuation would be
13. Kt—KKt5, with a very
strong attack—much clearer than
13. R—K1, Kt—QR4; 14. Kt ×
P, Kt × Q, etc.

13. B × B   P × B
14. Q × P ch   Kt—K2
15. Kt × B   P × Kt
16. KR—K1

Now that White controls the
open K-file as well his attack
must speedily become overwhelming.

16. ....   Kt—Kt1

Or 16. .... P × Kt; 17. QR—
Q1, Kt—Q2; 18. B × Kt and wins.

17. Kt—Q5

According to Maróczy in his
book *Paul Morphy* 17. B × Kt
would have been an easier win;
e.g.

A. 17. .... Kt × B; 18. Kt—
Q5, etc.

B. 17. .... Q—Q2; 18. Q—Kt3,
Kt × B; 19. Kt—Q5, etc.

17. ....   Q—Q2
18. B × Kt?

One of the rare instances of
Morphy slipping up in an attacking position. There was a whole
string of winning moves: 18. Q—
K5, 18. Q—K4, 18. Kt × Kt, or,
simplest of all, 18. Q × Q ch, K ×
Q; 19. Kt × Kt, etc.

18. ....   Q × Q
19. R × Q   K—Q2!
20. QR—K1   R—K1!

In this way Black regains his
lost piece, thanks to the pin on
the Bishop and the unsafe position of the Knight. The threat
of 21. .... P—B3 is unanswerable.

21. R(6)—K4   P—B3
22. R × P   P × Kt
23. R × P ch   K—B3
24. R—Q6 ch   K—B2
25. R—B1 ch   K—Kt1
26. B—R4

White has had to repay all his
material winnings, but he still
has a shade the better of it. The
rest of the game is not relevant to
our present subject. Suffice it
to say that Morphy won the ending in another 17 moves.

GAME 10

*One of Morphy's immortal combinations. Though displaying no
particularly deep planning this is an uncommonly charming game.*

White: P. MORPHY   Black: CHARLES, DUKE OF BRUNSWICK in
consultation with Count Isouard.

Paris, 1858.   *Philidor's Defence*

1. P—K4   P—K4
2. Kt—KB3   P—Q3
3. P—Q4   B—Kt5

An inferior line. 3. .... Kt—
KB3, 3. .... Kt—Q2, or even
3. .... P × P are all better than
this.

4. P × P   B × Kt

Otherwise a pawn is lost.

5. Q × B   P × P
6. B—QB4

The weakness of 3. .... B—
Kt5 is apparent. White is better
developed, has the two Bishops
and is already making serious
threats.

6. ....   Kt—KB3?

Black prevents the mate but
overlooks White's other threat.
6. .... Q—K2 was essential, so
as to meet 7. Q—QKt3 with
7. .... Q—Kt5 ch.

7. Q—Kt3

Winning at least a pawn.

7. ....   Q—K2

This is still the best move.
After 8. Q × P Black would play
8. .... Q—Kt5 ch and still be
able to put up a good fight in the
ending.

8. Kt—B3

Quite rightly White reckons
his attacking chances to be
worth more than a pawn. There

is now a real threat of 9. Q × P,
which would bring an immediate
decision.

8. ....   P—B3
9. B—KKt5

It now becomes clear how well
Morphy has judged his attacking
chances. His game is won.

9. ....   P—Kt4

Bad, but no worse than Black's
other possible moves:

A. 9. .... P—KKt3; 10. B ×
Kt, Q × B; 11. Q × P, and wins.

B. 9. .... P—KR3; 10. B ×
Kt, P × B; 11. 0—0—0, B—
Kt2; 12. B × P ch!, Q × B; 13. R—
Q8 ch, K—K2; 14. Q × P ch, K—
K3; 15. R—Q6 ch, and wins.

C. 9. .... Q—B2; 10. 0—0—0,
B—B4; 11. B × P ch, Q × B;
12. R—Q8 ch, K—K2; 13. Q ×
P ch, K—K3; 14. Q × Q ch, K ×
Q; 15. R × R, and wins.

D. 9. .... Kt—R3; 10. B ×
KKt, P × B; 11. B × Kt, P × B;
12. Q—R4. This way Black
extends his death struggle the
longest.

10. Kt × P!

An obvious enough sacrifice
which leads, however, to an uncommonly attractive finish.

11

10. ....   P × Kt
11. B × KtP ch   QKt—Q2
12. 0—0—0

Threatening B × Kt ch or R × Kt, with or without prior exchange on KB6.

12. ....   R—Q1

The only chance, as the following shows:

A. 12. .... Q—Kt5; 13. B × KKt!

(1) 13. .... Q × Q; 14. B × Kt mate.

(2) 13. .... P × B; 14. B × Kt ch, K—Q1; 15. B—B6 ch, etc.

B. 12. .... Q—K3; 13. B × KKt!; Q × B; 14. R × Kt, etc.

13. R × Kt!

Now it is plain sailing; not deep play perhaps, but exquisite.

13. ....   R × R
14. R—Q1   Q—K3
14. .... Q—Kt5 still fails against the reply 15. B × Kt! After the text move 15. B × Kt would also be sufficient, but White has something still prettier.

15. B × R ch   Kt × B
16. Q—Kt8 ch!   Kt × Q
17. R—Q8 mate.

A sparkling finish.

GAME 11

The pursuit of beauty was embodied in Anderssen. Many of his games show that he sought primarily the prettiest road and not necessarily the shortest. Morphy was guided rather by the rational ideas of today, according to which only the shortest road to any definite goal can be considered the prettiest. But the following game shows that he could also play deliberately for brilliancy.

White: H. E. BIRD   Black: P. MORPHY
London, 1858   *Philidor's Defence*

1. P—K4   P—K4
2. Kt—KB3   P—Q3
3. P—Q4   P—KB4

Morphy treading in Philidor's footsteps! But the move is not a good one.

4. Kt—B3
The strongest reply.

4. ....   BP × P
5. QKt × P   P—Q4
6. Kt—Kt3?

Nowadays it is known that the answer to Black's chosen variation is 6. Kt × P!, P × Kt; 7. Q—R5 ch, White getting an irresistible attack in return for the sacrificed piece.

After the text move Black has quite a good game.

6.	P—K5
7. Kt—K5	Kt—KB3
8. B—KKt5	B—Q3

Morphy has foreseen that the coming attack on his pinned Knight will turn out in Black's favour. Otherwise he would have played 8. .... B—K2.

9. Kt—R5	0—0
10. Q—Q2	

Not very good, for Black can easily defend himself against the threats of 11. Q—B4 and 11. B × Kt, P × B; 12. Q—R6. He should have played 10. P—KB4 or 10. B—K2.

10.	Q—K1!

This puts White into sudden difficulties, for he is faced with threats against both his Knights.

11. P—KKt4

This costs a pawn without compensation; but White had only a choice of evils:

A. 11. Kt × Kt ch, P × Kt; 12. B × P (the only move, for the Knight has no retreat), 12. .... R × B; 13. Q—Kt5 ch, R—Kt3; 14. Kt × R, P × Kt; 15. Q × QP ch, K—Kt2; and Black has the better of it because of his two Bishops. (Maróczy, in his Morphy book, judges the chances as even.)

B. 11. B × Kt,
  (1) 11. .... P × B; 12. Kt × P ch, etc., transposing into variation *A.*
  (2) 11. .... Q × Kt(R4);
    (*a*) 12. Q—Kt5, Q × Q; 13. B × Q, B × Kt; 14. P × B, Kt—B3; and Black wins the K-pawn.

    (*b*) 12. B—KKt5, Kt—B3; and Black has an excellent game.

11.	Kt × P
12. Kt × Kt	Q × Kt
13. Kt—K5	Kt—B3
14. B—K2	Q—R6
15. Kt × Kt	P × Kt
16. B—K3	R—Kt1

Black has a good position and a sound extra pawn. No present-day master would have much difficulty in winning from here by pure technique.

17. 0—0—0	R × BP?!

12

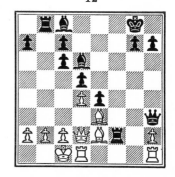

The quest for brilliancy. Black prefers not to play on for a dry win but plunges into a most surprising sacrificial combination —a combination however which is not quite sound, and which, if properly answered, should have yielded only a draw.

There was no need whatever to handle this position in a combinative style—certainly not without being absolutely sure that even against the strongest counterplay the chosen method would lead to complete success.

18. B × R	Q—R6!

This is the magnificent point of the Rook sacrifice. Black threatens mate on Kt7 and the Queen cannot be taken because of the reply 19. .... B × P mate. It is understandable that Morphy could not resist the temptation of this enchanting move, especially as White now has no easy way out.

19. P—B3
Other defences are insufficient; e.g.

A. 19. Q—B3?, B—B5 ch;
   (1) 20. K—Kt1, Q × Q; and wins.
   (2) 20. R—Q2, Q × RP;
      (*a*) 21.   Q—QR3,   Q × Q; 22. P × Q, P—K6; winning the Rook with decisive advantage to Black.

B. 19. Q—Kt5? Q × P ch; 20. K—Q2, B—Kt5 ch; 21. K—K3, Q—R6 ch;   22.   B—Q3,   B—R3!; 23. KR—Kt1, B—KB1; and Black's attack is irresistible.

19. ....   Q × RP
Threatening mate in two.

20. P—Kt4
If 20. Q—B2? Black wins by 20. .... B—B5 ch; 21. R—Q2, Q—R8 ch; 22. Q—Kt1, Q × Q ch (or 22. .... B × R ch).

20. ....   Q—R8 ch
21. K—B2   Q—R5 ch
22. K—Kt2?
An unjustified attempt to win. The proper move was 22. K—B1!, e.g.

A. 22. .... B × KtP; 23. P × B, R × P; 24. Q—B2, Q—R6 ch; 25. K—Q2, R—Kt7; 26. R—QB1, and Black is in trouble, for

his great pawn majority cannot be mobilized.

B. 22. .... Q—R8 ch, with perpetual check. This is the best line, but it means that with his pretty combination Black has thrown away the win.

22. ....   B × KtP!
With this second sacrifice Black gains a new and decisive advantage.

23. P × B   R × P ch
24. Q × R
Forced.

24. ....   Q × Q ch
25. K—B2
Other moves are even less adequate, for Black is now in a position to mobilize his pawn phalanx; e.g.

A. 25. K—R1, Q—R6 ch; 26. K—Kt1, P—K6; and Black wins by the double threat of 27. .... B—B4 ch and 27. .... P × B.

B. 25. K—B1, Q—B6 ch; 26. K—Kt1, P—K6; 27. B—K1, B—B4 ch; 28. K—R2, Q—B7 ch; and wins.

C. 25. K—R2, P—B4!
   (1) 26. P × P, P—Q5!; 27. B × P (or 27. R × P), B—K3 ch; 28.   K—R1,   Q—R6 ch; 29.   K—Kt1,   Q—R7 ch; 30.   K—B1,   Q × B; and wins.
   (2) 26. R—QKt1, Q—R5 ch; 27. K—Kt2, P × P; and Black wins easily.
   (3) 26.   KR—Kt1,   P—B5; (threatening   P—B6) 27. R—QKt1, Q—R5 ch; 28.   K—Kt2,   Q—Kt6 ch; 29. K—B1, Q—B6 ch; 30. K—Q1, B—Q2, and wins.

25. . . . .   P—K6!

Forcing a decisive intervention by the black Bishop.

26. B × P

Or 26. B—K1, B—B4 ch; and then:

A. 27. K—B1, Q—R6 mate.

B. 27. B—Q3, Q—B5 ch and wins.

26. . . . .   B—B4 ch
27. R—Q3

If 27. B—Q3, Black can win just the same by 27. . . . . Q—B5 ch.

27. . . . .   Q—B5 ch
28. K—Q2   Q—R7 ch
29. K—Q1   Q—Kt8 ch

and Black won.

GAME 12

The great secret of Morphy's astounding successes lay in his superior grasp of the general requirements of a position. It was essentially in this respect that Morphy towered head and shoulders above his contemporary, Anderssen. In the following game we make the acquaintance of Morphy as the consummate position player.

White: P. MORPHY   Black: D. HARRWITZ

Match, Paris, 1858.   *Philidor's Defence*

1.	P—K4	P—K4
2.	Kt—KB3	P—Q3
3.	P—Q4	P × P
4.	Q × P	Kt—QB3
5.	B—QKt5	B—Q2
6.	B × Kt	B × B
7.	B—Kt5!	

Thanks to the central formation, the so-called black half-centre (see *The Middle Game,* Part I, Chapter 10) White has a small edge in freedom of movement. In this game we shall watch Morphy make use of this slight advantage in unsurpassable style.

This fine seventh move prevents Black from completing his development economically with Kt—B3 and B—K2.

7.	. . . .	P—B3
8.	B—R4	Kt—R3
9.	Kt—B3	Q—Q2

Black has to keep in mind the weakness of his K3. If, for instance, 9. . . . . B—K2 White can take immediate advantage by 10. Q—B4, threatening Kt—Q4—K6.

10. 0—0

10. Q—B4 would achieve nothing now, because of 10. . . . . 0—0—0; 11. Kt—Q4, P—Q4! with about equal play.

10.	. . . .	B—K2
11.	QR—Q1	0—0
12.	Q—B4 ch	R—B2

A little trap. The natural continuation would have been 12. . . . . K—R1.

13. Kt—Q4!

This is stronger than the tempting 13. P—K5, threatening P—K6; e.g.

A. 13. .... QP × P?? This loses the Queen.

B. 13. .... BP × P? This loses the Exchange after 14. Kt × P.

C. 13. .... Q—Kt5! 14. R—Q4, Q—Kt3. If White then exchanges either on Q6 or B6 the result is equality: if, however, he plays 15. P—K6 his advanced passed pawn can become weak. Black was apparently counting on this last line when he played 12. .... R—B2.

13.	Kt—Kt5
14. P—KR3	Kt—K4
15. Q—K2!	

15. Q—Kt3, keeping up the pressure on K6, also came into consideration here, but in the long run the Queen is better placed on K2. As long as the position is not ripe for definite action one must prepare for all eventualities, and this is best achieved by a central placing of the pieces. This is the strategy to which the name 'centralization' was later given by Nimzovitch. In the application of centralization Morphy was unexcelled.

15. .... P—KKt4?

In difficult positions the mistakes occur of their own accord. The intention here is to prevent White from driving away the Knight, but it brings about a serious weakening of the K-side.

16. B—Kt3	R—Kt2
17. Kt—B5	R—Kt3
18. P—B4	

This is precisely the advance that Black was trying to rule out when he played 15. .... P—KKt4.

18.	P × P
19. KR × P	K—R1

Black has maintained his Knight on K4 and moreover has the open Kt-file at his disposal. His hope of counter-play, however, is not fulfilled, for the white Knight on B5 is even stronger than the black one on K4; under these circumstances the open Bishop-file is much more promising than the Knight-file.

Whoever is under pressure should prevent the opening of lines. This axiom is prettily borne out in the present case.

20. R—R4!

Threatening 21. B × Kt, BP × B; 22. R × P ch, K × R; 23. Q—R5 ch.

20. .... B—B1

There is no better defence; e.g.

A. 20. .... QR—KKt1??; 21. R × P ch, K × R; 22. Q—R5 ch, R—R3; 23. Q × R mate.

B. 20. .... Q—K1?; 21. B × Kt, QP × B; 22. R × P ch, K × R; 23. Q—R5 ch, K—Kt1; 24. Kt × B ch, with a won endgame for White.

21. B × Kt! BP × B

The strong Knight at Black's K4 has been eliminated, and the open files on the K-side turn decisively in White's favour.

22. R—KB1	Q—K3
23. Kt—Kt5!	

A very fine move, the object of which is to prevent Black from achieving a consolidated position by 23. .... Q—Kt1. In the first place there is now a threat of 24. Kt × BP, winning the Exchange.

23. ....   Q—Kt1

There is no real freeing move to be found; e.g.

A. 23. .... Q—Q2; 24. Q—R5!

(1) 24. .... B × Kt; 25. Q × R, B × R; 26. K × B, and Black is just about stalemated (26. .... R—K1?; R × P ch, or 26. .... R—Q1; 27. Q—B6 ch!).

(2) 24. .... K—Kt1; 25. Kt—B3, and White is lord and master of the position.

B. 23. .... B × Kt; 24. Q × B. This exchange brings out another nicety of 25. Kt—Kt5! Black is now left with his bad Bishop on B1 against the mighty Knight on KB5 and thus with a game already lost positionally. This last variation, however, would have provided the longest resistance.

24. R—B2

Answering the threat of 24. .... B × Kt followed by 25. .... R × P ch. After 24. Kt × BP Black would regain his pawn with an improved position: 24. .... R—B1; 25. Kt—Q5, B × Kt; 26. P × B, Q × P; 27. R × P ch, K × R; 28. Q—R5 ch, B—R3; 29. Q × R ch, K × Q 30. Kt—K7 ch, K—Kt2; 31. Kt × Q, R × P, etc.

24. ....   P—QR3

This leads to the loss of a pawn but 24. .... B × Kt; 25. Q × B, with the double threat of 26. Q × KtP and 26. Q—Q7 would have brought with it even greater disadvantages.

25. Kt × BP   R—B1
26. Kt—Q5   B × Kt
27. P × B   R—B2

If 27. .... Q × P there would follow 28. R × P ch, K × R; 29. Q—R5 ch, B—R3; and now:

A. 30. Q × R ch. This leads only to an equal ending for after 30. .... K × Q; 31. Kt—K7 ch, K—Kt2; 32. Kt × Q, R—B4! the Knight cannot move from Q5 for fear of 33. .... B—K6, so that White is compelled to give back his extra pawn with 34. P—B4. (Compare the note on 24. R—B2.)

B. 30. Kt × B!, R × Kt (forced); 31. Q—B5 ch followed by 32. Q × QR, and White has maintained his pawn with an overwhelming position. This variation is possible because White does not have to reckon with the possibility of being mated on Kt2. (Again compare the note on 24. R—B2.)

28. P—B4   B—K2
29. R—R5   Q—K1
30. P—B5!

13

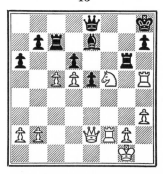

By profound positional chess Morphy has achieved a winning game. Now he calls upon his inspired combinative powers and forces a quick decision. The threat of 31. P × P, B × P; 32. Kt × B, R × Kt; 33. R × P, putting White two pawns up, confronts Black with an insuperable problem.

30. ....   R × BP

After 30. .... P × P; 31. Q × P ch wins the Q-Rook.

31. R × P ch   K × R
32. Q—R5 ch   K—Kt1
33. Kt × B ch

Only now is the true purpose of 30. P—B5 revealed: the Bishop has lost the protection of the Rook which stood at QB2.

33. ....   K—Kt2

Or 33. .... Q × Kt; 34. Q × R ch, and White wins the Queen. (34. .... K—R1; 35. R—B7, or 34. .... Q—Kt2; 35. Q—K8 ch, K—R2; 36. R—B7.)

34. Kt—B5 ch   K—Kt1
35. Kt × P   Resigns.

A most masterly performance. In no single respect could Morphy's play in this game be improved.

POSITIONAL PLAY
Steinitz (1836–1900)

THAT WHICH Philidor had sensed but through lack of combinative talent had been unable to demonstrate convincingly; that which on the other hand Morphy had intuitively mastered to perfection but because of his dominant powers of combination had seldom needed to use as his main weapon—namely the systematic building up of the position by small scientific stages—this was worked out and codified by Steinitz in his theory of position play.

Position play implies the gradual strengthening of one's game and the avoidance of all risk. It is the art of inducing weaknesses in the opposing game without creating any in one's own. It is the fight to maintain material equilibrium or to upset it in one's own favour. It is the quest for points of contact for an attack.

We subdivide this important Steinitz chapter thus:

A. His Career
B. His Teachings
C. Elucidation of his Teachings
D. Games played by Steinitz

A. HIS CAREER

Wilhelm Steinitz was born on the 14th May, 1836 in Prague. He was one year older than Morphy—from whom, however, he must have learned a great deal. By the time Steinitz was beginning to devote himself to chess seriously in 1862 Morphy's chess career was over. It goes without saying that a man with the analytical capabilities of Steinitz must have subjected the games of his most famous contemporary to a searching examination. We mention this because it is a link which has been neglected in most treatments of the history of chess.

In his first period Steinitz was wholly a combinative player, and a very successful one, even though he never quite reached the heights attained by Anderssen and Morphy.

After a few years in Vienna Steinitz came, in 1862, to England, and it was here that he began to think along positional lines. However, it was a slow process: even in 1866 when he succeeded in winning a match against the great Anderssen by 8–6 Steinitz was by no means a purely positional player. One striking thing, though, was his proficiency in the realm of defence. It soon became apparent that Steinitz was winning his games by refuting the sharp attacks launched by his opponents. In his own attacks he went to work more prudently, making less use of the gambits and beginning to prefer such solid, quiet openings as the Ruy Lopez and Queen's Gambit.

Steinitz entered his great period in 1872 when he became chess editor of *The Field*. In a position now to put his ideas on paper, and fortified by a large circle of readers, he found his true vocation as a chess thinker and chess teacher. Later on, from 1885 to 1891, Steinitz also ran his own chess periodical, *The International Chess Magazine*. Thus he became the most prolific chess writer of the 19th century, and the preacher of a new doctrine which was not fully grasped until after his death.

In contrast to Philidor, Steinitz possessed the playing strength to demonstrate the correctness of his teachings; and unlike Morphy he had the means of sharing his ideas with the chess world. Of these three founders of position play, therefore, Steinitz is far and away the most important.

From 1873 to 1882 Steinitz worked almost exclusively on his theories and seldom took part in any tournament play; but in 1882 and 1883 he put his ideas to the test in two great tournaments. The results were somewhat disappointing. In the tournament of Vienna, 1882 it was no sensation that such a prominent master as Steinitz should come out top; but that he should have to share top place with Winawer, a tactician who did not wholly approve of the Steinitz teachings, this was not exactly flattering to the prophet of position play. Still worse was to come at the London Tournament of 1883. Zukertort, a very gifted combination player—though not one of the wilder sort—came first by a margin of three (!) points, and Steinitz had to be content with 2nd prize.

Was position play then after all no *sine qua non* for the complete chessplayer? Must it be considered only a matter of using scientific method as a substitute for original talent? By no means, though Steinitz did as a rule put too much faith in his position play and tended to leave combination out of the reckoning, and his results suffered accordingly.

In 1886, however, Steinitz achieved the success of his life when he defeated the highly gifted Zukertort by 10–5 in a match. It was a triumph not only for his theories but also for his essential qualities of character—tenacity and grim determination. When Zukertort started off by taking a 4–1 lead Steinitz was undismayed and only proceeded to exert his own playing strength to the full. 'The one who was the greater thinker won the day from the one who had the greater talent' was the way Lasker summed up the match.

After his match victory over Zukertort Steinitz proclaimed himself world champion, and the chess world readily agreed, on the understanding that any person who could defeat him in a match should take over the title. Steinitz successfully defended his title three times, beating Chigorin 10–6 in 1889; Gunsberg, also 10–6, in 1890; and Chigorin again, this time 10–8, in 1892. The games of these matches give one the impression that Steinitz could have won by wider margins if he had paid more attention to the tactical side of the game; but in pure strategy these masters were not of the stature of Steinitz.

He lost the world title in 1894 to a player of balanced capabilities —a thorough strategist and at the same time a fine tactician— Emanuel Lasker. He defeated Steinitz 10–5 and in the return match two years later increased his margin to 10–2. In both cases superior tactics carried the day. Lack of a clear-cut attitude to combinative chess weighed heavily against Steinitz, especially in his later years.

In the mammoth tournament of Vienna, 1898, with 36 games to be played, mostly against prominent masters, it was another fine achievement for the 62-year-old Steinitz to win 4th prize. In the Cologne tournament of 1898 he again did well, finishing 5th. But by now his powers were rapidly waning. His last effort was unavailing: in the London tournament of 1899 he had to be content with 11th place.

Bitter disappointment, and perhaps also the dread that his failures might be attributed to his doctrines, had brought on neuroses, and on the 12th of August, 1900 the greatest chess preceptor in the history of chess died in New York.

B. His Teachings

Steinitz grew up in the palmy days of gambit play and was initially a gambit player himself, though not a particularly enthusiastic one. His critical bent soon led him to doubt the soundness of the gambits. During many of the incisive attacking games which he won he got the impression that he had really had the inferior position and had won only by grace of his opponents; and even though this grace was frequently vouchsafed—involuntarily of course, in the form of faulty defence—it afforded little satisfaction to Steinitz.

One should strive for attack, to be sure; but, Steinitz concluded, the attack should begin only when the position is ripe for it. Otherwise the eventual repulse of the attack will bring with it positive advantages for the opposition. Now the initial position is certainly not 'ripe for attack', and Steinitz therefore disapproved on principle of going all out for attack in the opening stages and sacrificing material to that end.

Steinitz laid down the principle of positional equilibrium. In general, advantages for both sides can be found in any position. So long as these advantages more or less cancel each other out the position is in equilibrium. Each player should seek to minimize the defects of his own position—for example by improving the placing of the pieces or by dissolving a doubled pawn—and at the same time to build up his own advantages. All the time one should be striving to upset the balance of the position in one's own favour, patiently biding one's time the while. At this stage forcing operations usually lead to disadvantage.

In positions of equilibrium correct play will automatically lead to new positions of equilibrium. The balance will be destroyed not by one's own good play but rather by misjudgments on the part of one's opponent. This belief implies a direct challenge to the previously held opinion that any position could be taken by storm if only one were a good enough player; that is to say, if one knew how to destroy the balance of the position by the power of one's own play.

Furthermore, Steinitz taught not only that it is incorrect to attack before the balance of the position has been significantly upset, but that when that moment comes one not only *may* attack, but *must*, otherwise the advantage will be lost. Dr. Lasker saw in this notion a great philosophical conception on the part of Steinitz.

Experience confirms this *must*. If one vacillates and continues to hesitate when the opportunity offers, it is noticeable that the attempt at further build-up quickly loses momentum and the tide of battle begins to flow the other way. One must strike while the iron is hot.

Steinitz advises the attacker to keep hammering away at the weakest point in the enemy position. To the defender his chief counsel is to avoid exaggerated passivity, and to refrain from weakening pawn moves.

To explain correctly how these general rules are applied is no easy task, but this is the problem to which we now turn, with the help of some examples.

C. Elucidation of his Teachings

The fundamental principle of Steinitz reads: Make a plan which conforms to the needs of the position.

These needs are defined by various characteristic features: 'lead in development', 'strong centre', 'open files', etc. Steinitz taught that one should try to pick up such advantages one by one, no matter how tiny they may be, in preparation for launching the attack. (This is the so-called theory of accumulation.)

The characteristics of the position may be transient or of more lasting nature; at one moment they may require some immediate drastic action; at another, only solid manœuvring aimed at maintaining some advantage already gained. We give separate attention to some of the most important of these characteristics, and under C.11 we also give two examples to illustrate the conversion of temporary advantages into permanent ones.

Where the examples in this section are taken from actual play they do not include any examples at all played by Steinitz himself; they are from the games of later players who, consciously or unconsciously, have followed in his footsteps. The manner in which Steinitz put his principles into practice in his own games is the subject of section D of this chapter.

C.1. *Lead in Development*

Here we can be brief. The temporary nature of the advantage is self-evident, for a player can do no more than develop all his pieces, after which the arrears will automatically be wiped out. In due course the opponent will also complete his development unless there is some way of permanently preventing him, and this, of course, is highly unlikely.

A lead in development therefore lends itself primarily to conversion into something more lasting. The quick accumulation of advantages will then often bring the opportunity to launch an immediate K-side attack.

C.2. *Superior Mobility*

This feature is one of the most important of all. Obviously the pieces must be placed so as to command as many squares as possible and thus achieve maximum mobility.

In this concept the Bishops are especially involved, for Bishop mobility is closely related to the placing of the pawns—particularly the centre pawns. Just like Philidor, Steinitz drew attention to the fact that a Bishop can be 'good' or 'bad'. This fact stems from the existence of blocked pawns and depends on whether one's own blocked pawns obstruct the Bishop. When one has a single Bishop running on white squares, it is good to put one's pawns on black squares and correspondingly bad to have them on white.

In positions where many pawns remain on the board (and therefore particularly in the opening) there is another criterion to be distinguished concerning the bad Bishop—namely whether it stands inside or outside the pawn chain; i.e. before or behind its own fixed pawns.   (See Diagram 14.)

(Bad Bishop outside and inside the Pawn Chain)

In the diagram the two K-pawns are fixed for the time being, so that both the K-Bishops are theoretically bad. But White's is the better of the two, for a Bishop on QB4 will be outside the pawn chain, while a Bishop on K2 will be inside. The consequence of White's active Bishop position is that Black may be induced to exchange his good Q-Bishop for White's bad K-Bishop (e.g. by B—K3). On the other hand White will seldom want to exchange his good Q-Bishop for Black's bad Bishop on K2.

14

All things considered, White has rather the better of the position in Diagram 14.   The advantage is only marginal however, and will disappear completely if Black, after playing P—Q3, manages later on to force P—Q4.

To make this advance difficult for Black to achieve, White would do well to play P—Q4 rather than P—Q3, the idea being to open the Q-file and so control the square Q5 with more pieces than Black. True, the advance of a white pawn to Q4 gives Black the opportunity to dissolve his own K-pawn and then later on to get his K-Bishop outside the pawn chain via KB3; but this freeing operation may prove troublesome to carry out.   Game 12 can be consulted as an example of White playing P—Q4 in a situation like Diagram 14.

The difference in value between the good and bad Bishops becomes more marked as more pawns are fixed on the colour in question, and also as more of the other minor pieces are exchanged.   A clear-cut example is shown in Diagram 15.   White still has a theoretical possibility of playing his bad Bishop from Kt2 via B1 to Q3, thus either getting it outside the chain or exchanging it against Black's good Bishop; but to realize this plan is not going to be easy.

(The difference between good and bad Bishop in acute form)

15

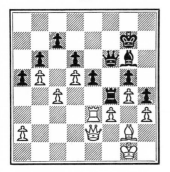

It is to be further observed that the scanty mobility of a bad Bishop usually becomes still more serious when it finds itself opposed to a Knight. This would be true for instance if in Diagram 15 the piece on Black's KKt3 were a Knight.

C.3. *Occupation of the Centre*

The forerunners of Steinitz were just as convinced of the importance of the pawn centre as was Steinitz himself. The difference lay in the use to which this centre was put. Whereas for Steinitz the pawn centre had both dynamic and static significance, the natural combination players considered it almost exclusively as a weapon of attack.

The central formation is quite frequently only temporary; fixed formations are the exception. We content ourselves here with one example of the neutralization of the centre.

(Neutralization of the centre)

16

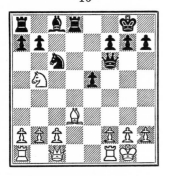

Black has a slight advantage here because of his occupation of the centre with his K-pawn; but White, to move, plays 1. P—KB4! compelling the exchange of the K-pawn, neutralizing the central situation and producing an approximately equal game.

C.4. *Unsafe King-position*

The King's security depends on the number of attacking possibilities. In most cases an unsafe King-position is a temporary feature, for in the long run, given sufficient time for consolidation, the King will always find a safe place. The chief difficulty arises when the castling privilege has been forfeited or—what amounts to the same thing—when the position of the wing pawns has been weakened. After castling, the safety of the King depends as a rule on the three wing pawns in front of the King; any move or exchange of one of these pawns lessens the resistance of that flank and thus decreases the security of the King.

With regard to these cases Steinitz warned the attacker against being too optimistic. 'The King is a strong piece' he used to say, meaning that this piece is quite capable of attending to its own safety. The games of Steinitz contain many daring examples of self-defence on the part of the King—witness for instance the Steinitz Gambit: 1. P—K4, P—K4; 2. Kt—QB3, Kt—QB3; 3. P—B4, P × P; 4. P—Q4, Q—R5 ch; 5. K—K2. Here the insecurity of the white King is more apparent than real. Steinitz had many successes with this opening, chiefly because his opponents considerably overestimated Black's attacking chances.

Nevertheless it is generally a dangerous thing to have one's King insecurely placed. Diagram 17 shows what we may call a borderline case.

(Unsafe K-position: a borderline case)

17

Black threatens 1. .... B × P and if then 2. B × B? Black will have a quick win by 2. .... Kt—B5! But White can eliminate the main danger at once by 1. Kt—K2 and then move his King into safety, after which the open KKt-file will be more of an asset than a liability.

C.5. *Weak Squares*

The doctrine of weak squares is one of the most important elements in the theories of Steinitz. By a weak square we mean one in or near one's own territory which can, in the long run, be occupied by a hostile piece. Obviously such occupation will have unpleasant consequences, for a piece which penetrates in this way is likely to command many points in the enemy ranks.

An invading piece will generally encounter great difficulties if both sides have kept the squares in their own territory more easily and safely accessible to their own pieces than to those of their opponent. Only in exceptional circumstances will it be possible for a piece to settle down successfully inside enemy territory, and then the explanation will usually be found in some uneconomical deployment of the opposing pieces and pawns.

Here are a few examples to explain the notion of a weak square.

(Weak square at Black's QKt3 caused by inappropriate placing of the black pieces)

18

This position, from a game Euwe–Colle, Paris, 1924, arose from a Sicilian Defence, Scheveningen Variation. Black had already played P—QB4 and P—QR3, depriving his QKt3 of all possibility of pawn defence, and he should have taken this into account in the placing of his minor pieces; this he had neglected to do. The game proceeded:

1. Kt—Kt3
Threatening to win the Exchange by 2. B—Kt6. Now it is evident that the black pieces are badly arranged—the Queen on B2 in a diagonal line with the Rook on Q1, and no minor pieces available to defend QKt3 at a moment's notice should it become necessary.

1. ....   R—K1
Had Black been able to meet the threat by playing a Knight to Q2 there would have been nothing much in the position; but since he has to take refuge in flight White gets time for a considerable strengthening of his attack against QKt6.

2. B—Kt6   Q—Kt1

3. P—R5   B—Q1
4. KR—Q1   Kt—QKt5
5. B × B   KR × B
6. Q—Kt6!   Kt—B3
Upon 6. .... Kt × BP there would follow 7. QR—B1, R—B3; 8. Q—B2, Kt—QKt5; 9. Q—Q4; winning the Knight.

7. Kt—R4   Kt—K1
8. P—QB4   Q—R2
9. P—B5!   P × P
10. Kt(3) × P   R—B2
11. R—Q2!
White's game is won, for the threat of QR—Q1 is unanswerable. For instance if 11. .... Q × Q, then 12. P × Q wins a piece. Black's position has collapsed simply on account of the weakness of his QKt3.

(Weak square at White's Q4 caused by his premature opening of the Q-file)

19

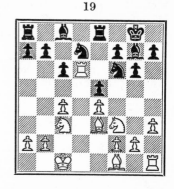

In this position (Tarrasch–Euwe, Pistyan, 1922) White's Q4 will be a lasting weakness. Black will eventually occupy this square with one of his Knights and thus obtain a clear advantage, for if White should ever exchange it off Black will be left with a strong passed pawn in its place.

The game continued: 13. B—Kt5, B—B1!; 14. R—Q2, K—Kt2; 15. B—Q3, B—Kt5; 16. K—B2, Kt—B4; 17. P—R3, B × Kt; 18. B × Kt ch, K × B; 19. K × B, R—Q1!; 20. B—B2, R × R; 21. Kt × R, Kt—K3; 22. P—KKt3, P—QR4; 23. Kt—B3, P—B4!; 24. B—R4, R—R3; 25. R—Q1, Kt—Q5! with great advantage to Black.

Weaknesses in the region of the King are in principle doubly dangerous, serving as they do for the basis of an attack on the King. Diagram 20 (Réti–Bogolyubov, Moscow, 1925) is a case in point.

(Black's K3 is a weak square in the neighbourhood of his King, and therefore doubly dangerous)

20

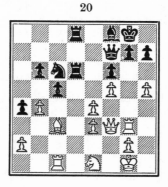

The continuation was:

1. P × P   P × P
2. P—R6   K—R1

3. P × P ch   B × P
4. Q—K2   Kt—Kt5?

Black should have striven by every possible means to prevent

White from getting a Knight to K6. The text move is a two-fold error: not only does Black permit the exchange of his Knight—the only piece which could have protected his K3—but also unguards his Q5, the very square from which the white Knight can get quickly to K6.

5. B × Kt   P × B

6. Kt—B3	P—Kt6
7. Kt—Q4	P × P
8. R—R1	B—R3
9. Kt—K6!	

Thanks to the commanding position of this Knight White now has a winning position. In the game Black could see nothing for it but to sacrifice the Exchange at his K3, but this led to no more than a stay of execution.

(Black's K-pawn is isolated and backward; in consequence his K4 square is very weak)

21

This position (from a game Spielmann–Colle) demonstrates the disadvantage of a backward and isolated pawn. If the black K-pawn were missing—e.g. in exchange for the white QB-pawn—there would be nothing much in the game. As it is, however, that K-pawn is a nasty obstacle to the freedom of movement of the black pieces, so that White is able to get a winning attack by occupying his K5.

1. P—Kt5   Kt—K2
Black could have put up a better fight with 1. .... R × Kt; 2. R × R, Kt × QP.

2. Kt—K5   R × R ch
Here again Black misses a chance to prolong the game: 2. .... Q—K1; 3. R × R, P × R; 4. Kt—Kt4, Q—Kt3; and White will still have to play very precisely. After the exchange of

Queens, for instance, White's B-pawn would be undefended.

3. R × R   Q—K1
4. R—B7
Now it is all over. The main threat is 5. B × P.

4.	Kt—B4
5. P—Kt4!	Kt × B
6. Q—Kt6!	and wins.

C.6. *The Pawn Position*

This also is one of the Steinitz fundamentals. To a certain extent it harks back to Philidor, who always set great store by the position of the pawns.

It was shown in Section C.5 that weak points come into being primarily through the position of the pawns, although it is the position of the pieces which confirms the weakness. In practice therefore a correct appraisal of the pawn position is of the greatest importance.

In the initial position the pawns are ideally placed: two closed ranks of eight with full freedom to move and ample opportunity for mutual defence. In this horizontal array they control both the black and the white squares and thus form an impenetrable wall of guarded squares.

No possibility exists of strengthening this original position of the pawns. They can only be weakened, for example, by reduction in numbers or by doubling. These alterations in the pawn set-up are organic weakenings.

Functionally, however—that is to say having regard to previously mentioned pawn-characteristics—it is possible not only to weaken but also to strengthen the initial arrangement. Consider the following moves, starting always from the original position:

White plays P—Q4 and P—K4; this is a functional strengthening (occupation of the centre).

Black plays P—KB3 and P—KR3; this is a functional weakening of the black K-side.

White captures on QKt3 with his R-pawn; this produces a slight organic weakening (doubled pawn!) but at the same time a small functional strengthening (open R-file!).

Black captures on KR3 with his Kt-pawn; this involves a serious organic weakening, destroying the unity of the pawn mass (isolated doubled KR-pawns). Functionally there may be a slight strengthening, if the open Kt-file can play any part in the game.

Organic weaknesses are likely to be permanent and to bring functional weaknesses in their train. As for purely functional weaknesses, they may be either temporary or permanent according as the pawns concerned are free or fixed.

Finally it is necessary to distinguish between weak pawns and weak squares in the vicinity of the pawns. The expression 'weakness' usually refers to a weak square (see positions 19, 20 and 21). Such weaknesses are usually the cause of the weakness of the pawn itself.

For further examination of the relative importance of various pawn formations we now subdivide as follows: (*a*) united pawns; (*b*) isolated pawns; (*c*) doubled pawns.

C.6(*a*) *United Pawns*

The ideal example of united pawns is the initial position. After 1. P—K4 this pawn has given up its influence on the squares Q3, Q4, KB3 and KB4 once for all; but this is of no consequence, for these squares can still be guarded by the QB-pawn or the KKt-pawn. If, however, we remove the QB-pawn from White's original array, then after 1. P—K4 the squares Q3 and Q4 are permanently deprived of any pawn protection, so that the Q-pawn lacks the comforting support of a colleague unless it can be advanced to Q5.

Now going back to the original position again, if we remove the white QB-pawn and the black QR-pawn, then Black stands the better, for there is less danger that the advance of one of his pawns will leave weak squares in his position. (From this point of view compare the consequences of the move 1. P—K4 by White with those of 1. .... P—K4 by Black.) This leads to the important conclusion that a number of pawns which form one unbroken group (in the present case Black's QKt2 to KR2) are preferable to the same number split into two or more groups (in the present case White's QR2 and QKt2, and Q2 to KR2)—other things, of course, being equal.

The value of a pawn formation depends primarily upon whether the pawns are united or not. If they are, then, exceptional cases apart, they are best arranged horizontally. Oblique or zig-zag formations have the fundamental disadvantage that they guard only one colour, so that neighbouring squares of the other colour are liable to become weak.

For instance from the initial position (and ignoring for the moment the actions of the pieces) suppose we make the following moves: 1. P—K4, P—K4; 2. P—KB3, P—KR4; 3. P—KR3, P—R5. White's zig-zag K-side formation now contains gaping weaknesses on KB4 and KKt3, and two dynamically fixed (i.e. backward) pawns on KB3 and KKt2. The whole formation K4—KB3—KKt2—KR3 is crippled, and can be held in restraint by only two black pawns— evidence of how the value of united pawns can be reduced by the unwarranted setting up of a diagonal formation (refer to Game 3, and read the note to White's 11th move).

C.6(*b*) *Isolated Pawns*

Any pawn which has lost contact with its comrades can easily be threatened by enemy pieces, especially from the front, and is therefore likely to become weak. But this is not the only danger. Equally serious is the fact that the square in front of the isolated pawn is preeminently eligible for occupation by a hostile piece. This has already been illustrated.

It does remain to be said, however, that the question of which half of the board the square in front of the isolated pawn is in is not a matter of indifference.   Compare Diagram 21 with Diagram 22.

(White will occupy the blockade square Q4)

22

In Diagram 21 the black K-pawn was isolated.   White's blockade square K5 lay within the black camp and constituted a distinct weakness there.   But in Diagram 22 (Alekhine–Euwe, 1927) White's blockade square Q4 is within his own position.   It is, to be sure, an excellent post for the white pieces, but it can hardly be called a weakness in the black position.   There followed: 1. Kt—QR4, B—K2; 2. B—K3, Kt—K5; 3. R—B1, B—K3; 4. Kt—Q4, Kt × Kt; 5. B(3) × Kt, Q—R4; 6. P—B3, Kt—B3.   White's advantage is slight.

C.6(c) Doubled Pawns

A doubled pawn is always a permanent organic weakness; its practical significance, however, is not always very great.   Two sorts of doubled pawns are to be distinguished: united doubled pawns, which have one or two neighbours, and isolated doubled pawns, which have no neighbour.

The main disadvantage of a doubled pawn is that it reduces the attacking potential of the formation.   This drawback, however, usually makes itself felt in the endgame—that is to say as soon as it is a matter of creating a passed pawn.

Isolated doubled pawns are naturally a more serious liability than united ones.   The isolation always brings with it the danger that the doubled pawns may themselves become weak, and this begins to tell in the middle-game.

(*Types of doubled pawns and their drawbacks*)

23

In the diagram there are two sets of isolated doubled pawns (White's on the KKt-file and Black's on the K-file). Black also has doubled KKt-pawns, united to the KR-pawn.

The weakness of the isolated doubled pawns is not serious in the present case since, apart from the Kings, there are no pieces left to attack them; but the weakness of the black KKt-pawns is decisive.

The situation on the KKt- and KR-files is this: White's formation has the defensive power of two pawns but the attacking power of only one; Black's formation has the defensive power of three pawns but the attacking power of only two. Since Black must strive to convert his extra pawn into a passed pawn it comes about that he must match his own attacking power with White's defensive power, and these are equal, 2–2. The consequence is that White wins, for his majority on the Q-side can be realized, while Black's on the K-side cannot. From Diagram 23 White wins as follows:

1. P—QKt4	P—KR4
2. P—R4	P—Kt4
3. P—Kt4!	

Most important. After 3. P—Kt5? P—Kt5! Black would manage to draw; e.g. 4. P—R5, K—Q2; 5. K—Q2, P—Kt4; and the white King cannot leave the quadrangle of the KR-pawn.

3. ....   P—Kt3

Evidently there are no chances to be found in 3. .... P × P; or in 3. .... P—R5.

4. P—Kt5

After 4. P × P? P × P; or after 4. P—Kt3? the game is drawn, the white King again being tied to the quadrangle of the KR-pawn to provide against its possible advance.

4.	K—Q2
5. P—R5	K—Q3
6. K—Q2	K—Q2

Or 6. .... K—Q4; 7. P—R6 and wins.

7. K—B3, etc.

C.7. *The Q-side Majority*

The majority of pawns on the side not occupied by one's own King is a very important weapon in the middle-game. Such a majority can be advanced fast without any danger to one's King.

If the players have castled on opposite wings the possessor of such a majority will be thinking in terms of a mating attack. If, however, both have castled on the same side the advantage of the far-side majority consists in the possibility of creating a passed pawn capable of being well advanced in the middle-game—the opponent meanwhile being unable to return the compliment on the other wing because of the presence of the Kings. In practice such an active majority occurs almost exclusively on the Q-side, both sides having castled short.

The defending side must then strive either to launch a K-side attack with the object of delaying the advance of the Q-side majority by indirect means or else to reduce the game to an ending before the said majority has yielded a dangerous passed pawn; it will then be possible for the K-side majority also to advance quickly without danger, thus establishing positional equilibrium. Here is an example from the Capablanca–Marshall match, 1909.

(The realization of a Q-side pawn majority)

24

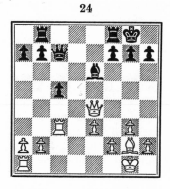

White has no compensation whatever for Black's Q-side majority. He can neither do anything on the K-side nor bring about an ending in time to save himself. Black (Capablanca) played:

18.	P—QKt4!	21. R—Q1	R × R ch
19. P—QR3	P—B5	22. B × R	R—Q1
20. B—B3		23. B—B3	P—Kt3

After 20. R—Q1, KR—Q1; 21. R(3)—B1, P—QR4; Black would also have had an overwhelming game; but after the text move it is even easier for him.

Stronger than 23. .... R—Q7; which would be met by 24. R—B2. There is now a threat of 24. .... B—Q4; 25. Q—Kt4, P—KR4; winning a piece.

20. .... KR—Q1
Thus Black obtains another important advantage—possession of the open Q-file.

24. Q—B6 Q—K4
After 24. .... Q × Q; 25. B × Q, R—Kt1; 26. K—B1 White could still put up some resistance. *Don't*

go into the endgame too early. This is the watchword when capitalizing a Q-side majority.

Black now threatens 25. .... R—Q7.

25. Q—K4
There is nothing better. If 25. R—B2 Black wins by 25. .... B—B4; e.g.

A. 26. R—K2, R—Q8 ch; 27. K—Kt2, B—Q6.

B. 26. P—K4, B—R6; 27. P—R4, Q—Q5!, etc.

25. ....   Q × Q
Now that White cannot recapture with gain of tempo (attack on the QKt-pawn) the exchange of Queens leads to an easy win.

26. B × Q	R—Q8 ch
27. K—Kt2	P—QR4
28. R—B2	P—Kt5
29. P × P	P × P
30. B—B3	R—Kt8
31. B—K2	P—Kt6
32. R—Q2	R—QB8
33. B—Q1	

Otherwise 33. .... R—B7 will be decisive.

33.	P—B6
34. P × P	P—Kt7
35. R × P	R × B

and Black won.

C.8. *Open Files*

We have repeatedly drawn attention to this feature. Let us recapitulate what we mean by open files. We refer to the vertical lines earmarked for Rook use. The horizontal lines are called ranks and the Bishop lines are diagonals.

A file is open when no pawn blocks it. If it is only one's own pawn which is missing, the opposing pawn being still present, we speak of a half-open file. The occupation of a half-open file is frequently more advantageous than the occupation of one which is fully open, for in the latter case the opponent will generally have the chance to occupy the file himself as well, and thus neutralize the situation. Occupation of an open file means nothing in itself: only when it is possible to prevent the opponent from occupying it as well can one speak of possessing the file.

In common parlance the term 'open file' is often used for half-open files as well.

The principal advantage accruing from the possession of an open file is that the Rooks will have a chance to penetrate to a rank inside enemy territory and there exploit their powers horizontally. The diagram makes this clear.

(Seizing and using an open file)

25

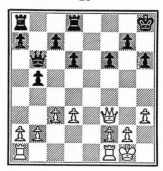

The continuation of the game from this position was:

1. KR—K1
Threatening 2. R—K7, which would give the Rook decisive horizontal influence.

1. .... R—K1
Black neutralizes the file, but only temporarily.

2. R—K3!
In order to double Rooks and thus completely possess the open file. This threat can no longer be parried, for the black Rook on K1 must protect his colleague on R1. (2. .... R×R? 3. Q× R(8) ch!)

2.	**QR—Q1**
3. QR—K1	**R—K4**
4. P—Q4	**R×R**
5. R×R	**Q—R3**
6. P—R3	**Q—B1**

Intending to neutralize the K-file once more by 7. .... R—K1.

7. Q—B6!
With the main threat of 8. R—K7, winning easily. After 7. Q—K2, Q—B4! 8. R—K7, R—Q2 Black would have been able to put up a better fight, his last move having restricted the horizontal activity of the white Rook.

7. .... Q—Q2
There is nothing better.

8. Q×Q	**R×Q**
9. R—K8 ch	**K—R2**
10. R—QKt8	

The Rook now exerts its full horizontal powers. White's game is won: he gains at least a pawn.

C.9. *The Advantage of the Two Bishops*

We have already remarked that two Bishops are usually stronger than Knight and Bishop or two Knights. This is just as true in the middlegame as in the ending. The superiority of the Bishops is most apparent when the position is open, so that they have enough diagonals at their disposal.

For further discussion of this subject the reader is referred to Game 21.

C.10. *Material Preponderance*

This permanent and most vital of all features requires no explanation. Suffice it to say that the value of any other feature whatever depends on the balance of material.

C.11. *Conversion of Temporary Advantages into Permanent Ones*

We mentioned this under the heading C.1. According to the teaching of Steinitz one should always be striving to accumulate advantages one by one, building up a lead that will serve as a sound basis for attack and combination. For this purpose permanent advantages are preferable on principle, and it is therefore important that temporary advantages should be converted into something more lasting.

This point is illustrated in the next two examples. In both cases we shall see how White, with the commonest of all temporary advantages—namely a lead in development—manages to create something of a more permanent nature.

(*Via lead in development to the win of a pawn*)

26

In this position (Alekhine–Tarrasch, St. Peterburg, 1914) White had managed, by a series of exchanges, to arrive at an important lead in development. The game proceeded:

1. R—Kt4!

After 1. Kt—Kt5, K—Q2! Black would have counterplay; e.g.

A. 2. Kt × BP, R—KB1! regaining the pawn with advantage, for 3. R—B4? fails against 3. ....
K—K2!

B. 2. Kt × RP

(1) 2. .... P—B3? 3. R—Kt4! winning a second pawn. (3. .... R—KKt1? 4. Kt × P ch!)

(2) 2. .... R—KR1; 3. R—R4, K—Q3. Here White

wins a pawn, it is true, but his position is uneasy.

| 1. .... | P—KKt3 |
| 2. R—R4! | K—K2 |

The R-pawn is not to be saved,

for 2. .... P—KR4 is met by 3. P—KKt4, etc.

| 3. R × P | R—Q1 |
| 4. R—R4 | R—Q4 |

In the matter of development the two games are now equal; but White has a sound extra pawn.

(*Via lead in development to the two Bishops and a superior pawn position*)

27

Here the actual number of pieces developed by the two sides is the same, but in the central build-up White has the advantage in that his Q-pawn and QB-pawn have been advanced. This tiny advantage is difficult to maintain; it can, however, be converted into something permanent. The game continued:

1. Kt—B4

With gain of tempo, through the attack on the K-pawn.

1.	P—Q3
2. P—Kt4	B—Kt3
3. P—QR4!	

Threatening to win the piece by 4. P—R5. After 3. Kt × B, RP × Kt; the white Bishop-pair would have little significance, for Black would have sufficient compensation in the open R-file.

| 3. .... | P—R3 |
| 4. Kt × B! | |

Thus White has killed two birds with one stone: he secures for himself the two Bishops and at the same time wrecks the black pawns.

| 4. .... | P × Kt |
| 5. Kt—Q2! | |

To maintain the Bishop-pair. The threat was 5. .... Kt—R4.

| 5. .... | P—KR4 |
| 6. P—B3 | |

Now, with two permanent advantages, White has an excellent game.

D. Games played by Steinitz

Now follows a selection of Steinitz games, characteristic of his style, his ideas, his courage and self-confidence—and also of his weaknesses. We see him as a great strategist producing magnificent attacking games when the nature of the position warranted that sort of treatment; but we also see him boldly go in for passages of laborious defence when he considered the opponent's attack to be unjustified. We see how he conceived and executed deep plans, sometimes creating advantages out of nothing; but we also see him endangering his game by various little inexactitudes. An ardent prophet of pure position play, Steinitz had a blind faith in his own general principles, and never cared what difficulties he might have to face when it was a question of defending the correctness of his ideas. Let the games speak for themselves.

Game 13

This is a fine attacking game. Characteristic of Steinitz, however, is the fact that he does not make purely attacking moves until the position justifies them.

White: W. Steinitz   Black: A. Mongredien

London, 1863.   *Double Fianchetto Defence*

1. P—K4	P—KKt3
2. P—Q4	B—Kt2
3. P—QB3	

Typical Steinitz. He makes no attempt to set up the broad centre which was certainly worth consideration here, but prefers a simple, solid formation.

3.	P—Kt3
4. B—K3	B—Kt2
5. Kt—Q2	P—Q3
6. KKt—B3	

Another characteristic move. Black has chosen a difficult defence—one which gives White various attacking possibilities. Many players would have chosen the incisive 6. P—KB4, and this would have given good chances. But Steinitz has another plan. For the present he does not consider the position ripe for sharp play.

6.	P—K4
7. P × P	

The positional point of this exchange will soon be apparent.

7.	P × P
8. B—QB4	

Thus, without any shadow of risk, White has achieved a favourable position. Because of the exchange of pawns the black K-Bishop, a bad Bishop inside its own pawn chain, is not a pretty sight. Moreover, the Q-Bishop has only limited mobility, White's K-pawn being easy to defend. The Q-file is open, but only White is able to occupy it easily.

8.	Kt—K2
9. Q—K2	0—0
10. P—KR4!	

After the quiet treatment of the opening this incisive move comes as a surprise, but it is fully justified by the present nature of the position. Black's P—KKt3 under the circumstances is seen to be a weakening and White means to take advantage of it to open the K-Rook file.

The more natural move 10. 0—0—0 would have allowed Black to play 10. .... Kt—Q2; and then after 11. P—KR4 he could have continued 11. .... Kt—KB3 with better defensive chances.

10. ....   Kt—Q2

Here Black should at least have played 10. .... P—KR3, so as to meet 11. P—R5 with 11. .... P—KKt4 and thus put off the opening of the file. This, it is true, would have created an ugly weakness at Black's KB4 and also provided White with the opportunity for a promising piece-sacrifice at his KKt5. However, the consequences of the move actually made are worse still.

11. P—R5   Kt—KB3
12. P × P   Kt × KtP

The alternative 12. .... RP × P is even less satisfactory; e.g.

A. 13. Kt × P. This is not the strongest, because of the reply 13. .... B × P! after which White has no decisive continuation. The sacrifice at KB7 is not on.

B. 13. 0—0—0! After this Black is doomed to hopeless passivity. A possible line would be: 13. .... Kt—B3; 14. Kt—Kt5, Q—K2; 15. P—KKt4, B—B1; 16. P—B3, Kt—Q1; 17. R—R4, B—K3;

18. QR—R1, B × B; 19. Q—R2, and White wins.

13. 0—0—0

Now that White has secured the permanent advantage of an open KR-file he finds time to castle.

13. ....   P—B4
14. Kt—Kt5   P—QR3

Black is intent on getting a counter-action of his own going, but he is much too late.

15. Kt × RP!

28

Only five moves after White's attack began the position is ripe for the decisive combination; and no wonder, for just about every white piece is placed more actively than its black counterpart, with the advantage of the open R-file in addition. White now wins by force.

15. ....   Kt × Kt
16. R × Kt

Here we see Steinitz still under the influence of Anderssen. He chooses the prettiest way rather than the most appropriate, which consisted of the simple 16. Q—R5, Kt—B3; 17. Q × Kt, threatening

18. B—R6. This would have been quicker than the move played, and would have led to an even greater material advantage; e.g.

A. 17. .... Q—B1;
   (1) 18. B—R6? Q—Kt5; and Black can still fight.
   (2) 18. R—R7! Kt × R; 19. B—R6 and White mates in three.

B. 17. .... B—Q4; 18. B × B, Q × B; 19. Q × B ch!, K × Q; 20. P × Q.

16.	K × R
17. Q—R5 ch	K—Kt1

18. R—R1	R—K1
19. Q × Kt	Q—B3
20. B × P ch	Q × B

Upon 20. .... K—B1 there would have followed 21. B × R, R × B; 22. R—R8 ch, B × R; 23. B—R6 ch, K—K2; 24. B—Kt5, winning the Queen.

21. R—R8 ch	K × R
22. Q × Q	

White has given two Rooks for the Queen, so that his advantage is only two pawns. But the win is certain for White also keeps the attack. Black resigns.

GAME 14

A twin to Game 13: the same features and the same consequences.

White: W. STEINITZ   Black: M. CHIGORIN

Match, Havana, 1892. *Ruy Lopez*

1. P—K4	P—K4
2. Kt—KB3	Kt—QB3
3. B—Kt5	Kt—B3
4. P—Q3	

Steinitz is satisfied with small advantages. He has placed his bad Bishop outside the pawn chain, and Black cannot very well follow suit. Most players give preference here to the sharper line 4. 0—0.

4.	P—Q3

Black shuts in his bad Bishop, for 4. .... B—B4 would (also) have brought distinct difficulties:

A. 5. B × Kt. This leads to nothing because of 5. .... QP × B! after which 6. Kt × P? fails against 6. .... Q—Q5!; 7. B—K3, Q × Kt; 8. P—Q4, Q × KP; 9. P × B, Q × KtP, etc.

B. 5. P—B3! The right answer.

White now really threatens B × Kt followed by Kt × P; and if Black plays 5. .... P—Q3 there follows 6. P—Q4 with clear advantage to White.

5. P—B3

To secure the Bishop on Kt5 against exchange. White is also in a position now to choose his moment to take the initiative in the centre by playing P—Q4.

5.	P—KKt3

Present-day opinion holds that 5. .... P—QR3; 6. B—R4, B—K2; 7. QKt—Q2, 0—0; followed by P—QKt4 and P—Q4 gives Black enough counterplay.

6. QKt—Q2	B—Kt2
7. Kt—B1	

As a rule Steinitz was in no hurry to castle. These tactics

had a significant effect in Game 13, and in the present case the point will also soon become clear.

7. ....   0—0
8. B—R4

But for this move Black would eventually have been able to exchange this Bishop.

8. ....   Kt—Q2

This is what justifies White's last move. With the Bishop still on Kt5 there would now be a little threat of Kt—Kt3 followed by P—QR3.

8. .... P—QR3 would, however, have been a better move for Black; e.g. 9. Kt—K3, P—QKt4; 10. B—Kt3 (10. B—B2, P—Q4!) 10. .... Kt—R4; 11. B—B2, P—B4; etc., with nice counterchances.

9. Kt—K3

The position calls for P—Q4 by Black. White keeps a continuous watch on this threat; his opponent, in this respect, plays less logically.

9. ....   Kt—B4

See the previous note. 9. .... Kt—Kt3 would have been a more systematic approach.

10. B—B2   Kt—K3
11. P—KR4!

The same kind of operation as in Game 13. White is going to open the KR-file, thus profiting both from his deferred castling and from his passive play in the centre which will have the effect of minimizing any counterthrust in that region by Black.

11. ....   Kt—K2

At last Black hits on the right

idea. After 11. .... P—KR3; 12. P—R5, P—KKt4; 13. Kt—B5 White would have a dominating game.

12. P—R5   P—Q4!
13. RP × P   BP × P?

Apparently in the hope of a counterattack on the KB-file, but this hope has no basis in reality. After 13. .... RP × P! Black would still have had reasonable chances of setting up a sufficient defence.

14. P × P   Kt × P
15. Kt × Kt   Q × Kt
16. B—Kt3

Now the weakness of 13. .... BP × P? appears. Instead of one favourable feature, the open R-file, White now has two, which reinforce one another—the R-file and the open Bishop diagonal from his QKt3 to KKt8. Positional equilibrium is thus seriously upset and the position is ripe for attack. Without waiting for the grass to grow under his feet Steinitz puts the enemy King under cross-fire.

16. ....   Q—B3
17. Q—K2   B—Q2
18. B—K3   K—R1

He quits the line of the Bishop but steps directly into the line of the Rook. Black is in great trouble.

19. 0—0—0

Late in the game White castles, and now with great effect.

19. ....   QR—K1
20. Q—B1

The Queen moves out of line with the black Rook on K1, preparing not only P—Q4 but also the rapidly decisive combination which follows.

20. ....   P—QR4

In order to drive the Bishop off his diagonal by 21. .... P—R5, but he gets no opportunity for this. 20. .... R—B4 would have been a little better.

21. P—Q4!   P × P

Forced, in view of the threat of 22. P—Q5.

22. Kt × P   B × Kt

Other continuations are also inadequate; e.g.

A. 22. .... Kt × Kt; 23. R × P ch! K × R; 24. Q—R1 ch and mate in two.

B. 22. .... Q—R3; 23. B—QB4, Q—R1; 24. Kt—B3 with a winning attack.

C. 22. .... Q—K5; to this move White has the choice of two favourable replies:
  (1) 23. Kt—B3, threatening 24. R × B as well as 24. B × Kt followed by 25. R × P ch and 26. Kt—Kt5 ch winning the Queen.
  (2) 23. B—B2, Q—Kt5 (the KKtP must be protected) 24. P—B3, Q—Kt6; 25. Kt—B5, P × Kt; 26. R × B, etc.

23. R × B

With threats all along the line.

23. ....   Kt × R

After 23. .... P—QKt4 White has the decisive 24. Q—Q3, with a double threat of 25. R × B and 25. Q × KKtP; e.g.

A. 24. .... Kt × R; 25. B × Kt ch, R—B3; 26. Q × KKtP, etc.

B. 24. .... Kt—B4; 25. R × P ch! K × R; 26. R—R4 ch, K—Kt2; 27. Q—Q4 ch, Q—B3; 28. B—R6 ch, K—R2; 29. B × R ch, Q × R; 30. Q—Kt7 mate.

24. R × P ch!

29

A sparkling finish, which lights up the real point of 20. Q—B1.

24. ....   K × R
25. Q—R1 ch   K—Kt2
26. B—R6 ch   K—B3

Otherwise 27. B × R ch, B—R6; 28. Q × B mate.

27. Q—R4 ch   K—K4
28. Q × Kt ch K—B4
29. Q—B4 mate.

*Here the pros and cons of an isolated Q-pawn form the theme. Steinitz
sets out to demonstrate the disadvantages and succeeds in masterly
fashion.*

White: J. H. ZUKERTORT   Black: W. STEINITZ

Match game, St. Louis, 1886. *Queen's Gambit*

1. P—Q4	P—Q4
2. P—QB4	P—K3

The Classical Queen's Gambit.

3. Kt—QB3	Kt—KB3
4. Kt—B3	P × P

Present-day opinion is that it is
inadvisable to accept the Classical
Queen's Gambit. 4. .... B—
K2; 4. .... P—B4; 4. ....
P—B3; or 4. .... QKt—Q2;
are all to be preferred.

5. P—K3

5. P—K4 is a more incisive
move. The text move trans-
poses into the normal Q-Gambit
Accepted, which usually arises
from 2. .... P × P.

5.	P—B4
6. B × P	P × P
7. P × P	

This voluntary isolation of the
Q-pawn, though not forced, does
constitute White's only chance of
getting any initiative. After
7. Q × P, Q × Q; 8. Kt × Q the
game is dead level.

7.	B—K2
8. 0—0	0—0
9. Q—K2	QKt—Q2
10. B—Kt3	Kt—Kt3
11. B—KB4	

The isolated pawn has the advantage of providing White with
a beautiful outpost for the Knight

on K5, and this should give
attacking chances. The logical
way of playing, therefore, was
11. R—Q1 and 12. Kt—K5,
followed by B—KKt5 or possibly
B—K3. The chosen move does
not fit into this plan. Instead it
enables Black to occupy the important blockade square at his
Q4 with gain of tempo, and thus
to get it securely in his possession.

11.	QKt—Q4
12. B—Kt3	Q—R4
13. QR—B1	B—Q2
14. Kt—K5	

Now this move serves no good
purpose.

14. ....   KR—Q1

Black can quietly invite the
exchange of his Q-Bishop. In
view of his isolated pawn White
must always play for attack and
consequently must as far as
possible avoid exchanges. By
15. Kt × B White would be
giving away the very piece which
is essential to his K-side activi-
ties. It follows that after
15. .... R × Kt the emphasis
would be on the disadvantages
of the isolated pawn.

15. Q—B3

With this move White does
threaten to acquire the two

Bishops under favourable circumstances: 16. Kt × Kt, P × Kt; (16. .... Kt × Kt??; 17. Q × P ch!) 17. Kt × B, etc.

15. ....   B—K1
Thus Black keeps possession of his blockade square Q4, for he can no longer be forced to recapture with the pawn.

16. KR—K1   QR—B1
17. B—KR4
A new attempt to force Black to recapture at Q4 with the K-pawn, and thus at least arrive at a symmetrical pawn position. The threat is 18. Kt × Kt (18. .... Kt × Kt? 19. B × B, Kt × B; 20. Q × KtP). The move is, however, an admission that White has only wasted time with B—KB4—Kt3.

17. ....   Kt × Kt
Surprising, and at first sight illogical, but in reality very good. Black is going to convert the favourable feature of his position—pressure against the isolated white Q-pawn—into another kind of advantage.

18. P × Kt   Q—B2
The pawn position is transformed but the prospects remain much as before. Instead of an isolated pawn on Q4 White has an isolated pawn-pair on the open Q- and QB-files, a formation which also has its own pros and cons. It is well adapted to supporting the pieces in an attack but from the defensive point of view is a liability. For such a pair of pawns Steinitz coined the striking name 'hanging pawns'.

The main good and bad points of hanging pawns are as follows: in horizontal formation (Q4, QB4) such a pair of pawns controls four squares on the fifth rank. Thus they hold the enemy pieces at bay and enhance the activity of their own. But they need continuous defence by pieces. The fact is that in horizontal formation *both* hanging pawns are destitute of pawn support. In oblique formation only one of them is in this state, but now there is the danger that the opponent will make himself master of the two blockade squares (i.e. with white pawns at Q4 and QB3 the squares at Black's Q4 and QB5).

A final disadvantage of the hanging pawns is their restricted 'exchangeability', for after the exchange of either the other one becomes an isolated pawn. Life is not easy for such Siamese twins!

19. Q—Q3
A move more likely to have caused trouble to Black would have been 19. B—Kt3.

19. ....   Kt—Q4
20. B × B
Here again 20. B—Kt3 could have been considered. Exchange of pieces suits Black very well.

20. ....   Q × B
21. B × Kt
See the previous note. 21. B—B2, to force a slight weakening of the Black K-side (21. .... Kt—B3; 22. Kt—Kt4) would still have kept attacking hopes alive.

21. ....   R × B

30

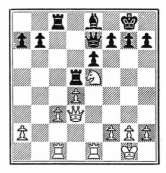

By now White has no attacking chances of any moment, but on the other hand his hanging pawns do not yet constitute a clear weakness. No vital error has been committed, and the chances are still about equal.

22. P—QB4
In principle this is the right move. The horizontal placing of the hanging pawns is certainly best, always provided that sufficient protection is available.

22. ....   R(4)—Q1
Not 22. .... R—R4, for this would separate the Rooks.

23. R—K3?
White is still out for K-side attack, but in view of the removal of three pairs of minor pieces and the lack of any point of contact this plan has no chance of succeeding and is decidedly mistaken.

White should have played to maintain positional equilibrium with such moves as KR—Q1 and then Q off the line of the black Rook—or possibly these moves in reverse order. Meanwhile he can keep in reserve the manœuvre P—QB5 followed by Kt—B4—Q6.

The text move deprives the hanging pawns of one important defensive possibility, and this may have serious consequences.

23. ....   Q—Q3!
24. R—Q1
If 24. R—R3 there could follow:

A. 24. .... Q × P; 25. Q × P ch, K—B1; 26. R—K3! with a promising game for White.

B. 24. .... P—KR3! 25. R—Q1, P—B3, etc., transposing into the actual game.

24. ....   P—B3
25. R—R3
A correct offer but an innocuous one, for Black can simply decline it. Other moves, however, would have been no better; e.g.

A. 25. Kt—Kt4. This sacrifice also gives results only if immediately accepted:
(1) 25. .... P—KR4;
   26. Kt × P ch,   P × Kt;
   27. R—Kt3 ch,   K—B1;
   28. Q—R7,   B—B2;
   29. R—Kt7 and White can still fish in troubled waters.
(2) 25. .... B—Kt3!; 26. Q—K2, P—K4! and Black wins with ease. (27. P—Q5, P—KR4!).

B. 25. Kt—B3, Q—R3! and Black wins at least a pawn with an overwhelming position.

C. 25. P—B5, Q—Q4; 26. Kt—B4, B—Kt4 and the hanging pawns will fall; e.g.
(1) 27. R—QB1, P—K4!, etc.

(2) 27.   Kt—Kt6,   P × Kt; 28. Q × B, P × P, etc.

25. ....   P—KR3!
After 25. .... P × Kt; 26. Q × P ch the white attack would be worth at least a draw; e.g.

A. 26.   .... K—B2? 27. R—B3 ch, K—K2; 28.   Q × P ch, B—B2; 29. Q × B mate.

B. 26.   .... K—B1; 27. R—KKt3!, etc.

26. Kt—Kt4
Threatening to sacrifice on B6 or R6 (compare the note to White's 25th move, variation *A*(1)).
If 26. Kt—Kt6 there could follow: 26. .... B × Kt; 27. Q × B, R × P;   28.   R × P,   Q × QP; 29. Q—R7 ch, K—B1; 30. Q—R8 ch, K—B2; 31. Q × R, Q × Q; and Black wins.

26. ....   Q—B5
Defending against both sacrifices and attacking the Knight.

27. Kt—K3   B—R5!
A fine move. By forcing the Rook from Q1 to Q2 Black creates opportunities to work with threats of mate on the back rank.

28. R—B3
An insignificant interpolation.

28. ....   Q—Q3
29. R—Q2
If 29. R × P Black settles the issue directly with 29.   .... B × R! Not, however, 29.   .... P × R; for then, after 30. Q—Kt6 ch, K—B1; 31. Q × BP ch, K—K1; 32. Kt—B5, P × Kt; 33. R—K1 ch, K—Q2; 34. Q—

B7 ch, K—B3; 35. R—K6, White can still fight.

29. ....   B—B3
30. R—Kt3
Other moves lead to nothing satisfactory; e.g.

A. 30. R × P, P × R; 31. Q—Kt6 ch, K—B1; 32. Q × BP ch, K—K1; 33. Kt—B5, P × Kt; 34. R—K2 ch, B—K5! and wins.

B. 30. P—Q5. This calls up difficult complications:
(1) 30.   .... P × P. Steinitz wrongly gave this as the refutation. Let us see:
(*a*) 31. P × P? Steinitz reckoned   only   with   this move, and gave Black to win as follows: 31.   .... B × P; 32. Kt × B, Q × Kt; 33. Q × Q, R × Q, etc.
(*b*) 31. Kt—B5! This gives White an irresistible attack; e.g.
   (i) 31.   .... Q—K4; 32.   R—Kt3,   Q—R8 ch; 33. R—Q1, etc.
   (ii) 31.   .... Q—Q2; 32.   R—Kt3, P × P; 33.   Kt × P ch   (or 33. Q × Q, etc., winning a piece) 33. .... K—R1; (or 33. .... K—B1; 34. Q—R7, etc.) 34.   Q—Kt6, R—K1; 35. P—KR4, mating or winning the Queen.
   (iii) 31.   .... Q—B1; 32. R—Kt3, P × P; 33.   Kt × P ch,   K—R1; 34. Q × R!, R × Q; 35.   R × R,   Q × R; 36. Kt—B7 ch., etc.
(2) 30.   .... Q—K4! This is

the right continuation and it wins at least a pawn for Black; e.g.

(a) 31. P—KR3, P × P; 32. P × P, B × P; 33. Kt × B, R—B8 ch; 34. R—Q1, R × R ch; 35. Q × R, R × P, etc.

(b) 31. P—Kt3, P—QKt4; 32. P × KtP, B × QP; 33. Kt × B, R × Kt, etc.

(c) 31. R—Kt3, P × P; 32. Q—Kt6, R—B2, etc. (33. Q × RP, Q × R!)

30. ....   P—B4!

31

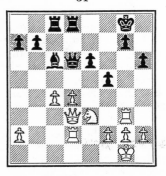

This counter-attack confronts White with an insoluble problem. It threatens 31. .... P—B5 winning a piece. The white Rook has achieved nothing on the K-side and now finds itself in a tight corner.

31. R—Kt6
A last attempt to keep hope alive by creating complications.

31. ....   B—K5
32. Q—Kt3   K—R2!
33. P—B5
This is the point of White's play; the Rook is rescued. But it makes no difference to the outcome of the game.

33. ....   R × P
34. R × KP
Or 34. Q × KP, Q × Q; 35. R × Q, R—B8 ch and now:

A. 36. Kt—Q1, B—B7 winning the piece.

B. 36. Kt—B1, B—Q4 followed by 37. .... B—B5, again winning the piece.

C. 36. R—Q1, R × R ch; 37. Kt × R, R × P with an easy win for Black.

34. ....   R—B8 ch
The weakening of the first rank induced by Black's 27. .... B—R5! now turns the scale.

35. Kt—Q1
Or 35. R—Q1, R × R ch; 36. Kt × R, Q × QP; and wins.

35. ....   Q—B5
36. Q—Kt2   R—Kt8
37. Q—B3   R—QB1
38. R × B
So that after 38. .... P × R? 39. Q × R, Q × R; he could give perpetual check by 40. Q—B5 ch, etc.

38. ....   Q × R(5)
Threatening Q—K8 mate. White resigns.

GAME 16

There is always an art in picking out from the multifarious aspects of a position just the ones which are going to influence the future course of events, and which therefore constitute the essence of the position. One feature can never be ignored—preponderance of material.

The value of a material advantage is often difficult to assess; the question arises, to what extent can the material be counter-balanced by some other type of advantage possessed by the other side? In doubtful cases Steinitz tended to come down on the side of the material advantage, often through habit or through obstinacy, for much of his life's work consisted of combating gambit play. In his attempts to refute gambits he never shunned any kind of danger. The hair-raising excursions he was prepared to undertake, and the dexterity with which he could defend an all-but-hopeless position, this game will show.

White: D. JANOWSKY   Black: W. STEINITZ
Cologne, 1898.   *Bishop's Gambit*

1.	P—K4	P—K4
2.	P—KB4	P × P
3.	B—B4	Kt—K2
4.	Q—R5	

This is stronger than 4. Kt—QB3, after which Black could play 4. .... P—QB3 and possibly 5. .... P—Q4 with a good game. After the text move Black does not achieve P—Q4.

4.	....	Kt—Kt3
5.	Kt—QB3	Q—K2

A most revealing move which runs counter to all the principles of sound development. Steinitz presumably reasoned as follows: 'Normal moves will get me nowhere, for White will at least easily regain the gambit-pawn with a good game; I don't propose to allow that without a struggle to anyone who has played a gambit; I would rather go under fighting. I intend anyhow to hold on to the gambit pawn for a long time. To this end my KB2 needs another defence, for 6. P—

Q4 will immediately threaten 7. QB × P. If however I defend KB2 by castling I am going to be mated; e.g. 5. .... B—Kt5; 6. Kt—B3, 0—0; 7. Kt—KKt5, etc. There is nothing for it then but this Queen move. It is not exactly pretty but my plan requires it. Let's get on with it then! I may even get in P—Q4 myself presently, for his K-pawn is now pinned.'

6.	P—Q4	Kt—B3
7.	Kt—B3	Q—Kt5

In the circumstances this is a fine move, and by it Black wins a tempo. It is also the only means of avoiding serious disadvantage. The white K-Bishop cannot move now because of 8. .... Kt × P.

8.	Q—Q5	Kt—Q1

Threatening to win a piece by 9. .... P—QB3.

9.	P—QR3	Q—K2
10.	0—0	P—Q3

Threatening 10. .... B—K3; 11. Q—QKt5 ch, P—B3; 12. Q—Kt3, B × B; with an important simplification for Black.

11. Q—KR5   P—QB3
Black thus succeeds in preventing the dangerous Kt—Q5. The net result of 7. .... Q—Kt5 can now be assessed. Black made two unproductive moves—Q—Kt5 and Q—K2—but White had to make three—Q—Q5, P—QR3 and Q—KR5.

12. B—Q2   Kt—K3
Black protects his forward KB-pawn once more and at the same time ties down the white K-Knight to the protection of the Q-pawn. 13. P—Q5 would be premature because by 13. .... Kt—B4; 14. QR—K1, Kt—Q2; Black would obtain full control of the important square at his K4.

13. QR—K1   Q—B2
14. P—Q5!   Kt—Q1
15. P—K5!
At last it is clear that Black's plan of campaign has been all too hazardous. By simple means White has built up a powerful position and now he goes over to direct attack.

15. ....   QP × P
16. Kt × P   B—B4 ch
17. K—R1   0—0
18. P × P   B—K6!
Black has a lost game but he puts up the best possible defence. Look at the other possibilities:

A. 18. .... P × P? 19. Kt × Kt, P × Kt; 20. Q × B, winning a piece.

B. 18. .... Kt × P? 19. Kt × KKt, etc., again winning a piece.

C. 18. .... Kt × Kt; 19. R × Kt with a winning attack; e.g. 19. .... B—Q3; 20. Kt—Q5, Q × P; 21. Kt—B6 ch! P × Kt; 22. R—Kt5 ch, K—R1; 23. Q—R6, P × R; 24. B—B3 ch, P—B3; 25. Q × BP ch, R × Q; 26. B × R mate.

19. Kt—B3?
In combinative style, but not the best. The simple 19. B × B was indicated; e.g.

A. 19. .... P × B; 20. Kt × Kt, P × Kt; 21. Q × P, Q × P; 22. Q—Q3, B—K3; 23. B—Q5! with a winning attack.

B. 19. .... Kt × Kt? 20. B(3) × BP, Kt(1) × P; 21. B—Q5! and White wins a piece.

C. 19. .... Q × Kt; 20. Q × Q, Kt × Q; 21. P × P! B × P; 22. R × P, Kt × B; 23. R × Kt and in spite of the Bishops on opposite colours White's extra pawn must be decisive, because of his great Q-side preponderance.

19. ....   B × B
20. Kt—KKt5
The logical continuation. After 20. Kt × B, P × P Black would suddenly find himself very well placed.

20. ....   P—KR3
21. Q × Kt   P × Kt
22. Kt—Q5   Q × P
23. Kt—K7 ch   K—R1
This is the critical moment. White's attack is just strong

enough to hold the game in equilibrium.

32

24. Q × P(Kt5)?
After this second mistake White loses. The right move was 24. B × P! with the following possibilities:

A. 24. .... Q × Q? 25. Kt × Q ch, K—R2; 26. Kt × R ch, winning the Exchange.

B. 24. .... B—B4? 25. Q × B, R × B; 26. Q—Q3, R × Kt; 27. R × R,
    (1) 27. .... B—K6; 28. R × B and wins.
    (2) 27. .... B—R4; 28. P—QKt4, B—Kt3; 29. P—Kt5 and wins.

C. 24. .... R × B? 25. Kt × Q and wins.

D. 24. .... Kt × B! 25. Kt × Q, B × R; 26. Kt—K7!, B—Q7;

27. Q—R5 ch, Kt—R3; 28. Kt—Kt6 ch, K—Kt1; 29. Kt × R, K × Kt; 30. P—KR4! with about equal chances. (30. .... P × P? would cost the black Bishop by 31. Q—QB5 ch, K—K1; 32. Q—K5 ch, K—B1; 33. Q—Q6 ch and 34. Q × B.)

    24. ....   Q—KR3
    25. Q—QB5
Threatening 26. Kt—Kt6 ch and 27. Q × R ch.

    25. ....   Kt—K3
    26. B × Kt   B × B
    27. R—K5   B—K6!
    28. Q—Kt5   P—KKt3
Here White could have quietly resigned. He is a piece short, and no glimmer of attack remains.

    29. Q × P   K—Kt2!
Threatening mate in three by 30. .... Q × P ch, etc.

    30. Q—B3   QR—Q1
    31. P—R3   Q—R5
    32. Kt—B6   B—Kt5!
    33. Q × B(4)
After 33. Q—K4 comes 33. .... B × P!

    33. ....   Q × Q
    34. P × Q   R—R1 ch
    35. R—R5   P × R
Resigns.

GAME 17

Nowadays it is almost a law that against a weaker opponent one should use sharp attacking methods. But these were precisely the cases in which Steinitz used to take no risk at all. Here he handles the opening in colourless style, yet before long he has obtained an overwhelming game simply through his better grasp of the general requirements of the position.

White: W. STEINITZ Black: B. FLEISSIG

Vienna, 1882. *French Defence*

1. P—K4	P—K3
2. P—K5	

Steinitz tried this somewhat premature advance several times.

2.	P—Q4

2. .... P—QB4, followed soon by P—Q3 would give better prospects of proving White's 2. P—K5 premature.

3. P × P e.p.	

Surprising. The Advance Variation, which would arise after 3. P—Q4, gives certain attacking chances at the cost of some positional risk. After the text move Black has an unusually easy game.

3.	B × P
4. P—Q4	Kt—K2

The one thing which demands Black's attention now is the liberation of his Q-Bishop—preferably by P—K4.

5. B—Q3	Kt—Kt3
6. Kt—KB3	Kt—B3

Not 6. .... P—K4? because of 7. B × Kt, etc., winning the pawn. After the text move Black's P—K4 is no more to be prevented. The game is level.

7. Kt—B3	Kt—Kt5

An aberration, caused by exaggerated respect for White's attacking Bishop. One notes how the idea of attack coloured all the thinking of players of the time. After 7. .... P—K4 there would have been nothing to choose between the positions.

8. B—QB4	P—QB3

A serious positional mistake, which shows that Black has not the faintest idea of the requirements of the situation. Instead of freeing his Q-Bishop he immures it completely within the chain of three pawns on QKt2, QB3 and K3.

It is true that 8. .... P—K4? is not playable because of 9. Kt—KKt5 (9. .... 0—0; 10. Q—R5 and wins) but 8. .... P—Kt3 or 8. .... P—QB4 would still have provided Black with a respectable game.

9. Kt—K4	B—B2
10. 0—0	0—0

10. .... P—K4 would now have been followed by 11. Kt(3)—Kt5 (11. .... 0—0; 12. Kt × RP! or 11. .. .. Kt—Q4; 12. R—K1).

11. R—K1	Kt—Q4

11. .... P—K4 would still

fail, this time because of 12. B—
KKt5! e.g.

A. 12. .... Q—Q2; 13. Kt—B5,
etc.

B. 12. .... Q—K1; 13. P × P,
Kt × KP; 14. Kt × Kt,
    (1) 14. .... Q × Kt; 15. Kt—
        B6 ch, etc.
    (2) 14. .... B × Kt; 15. Kt—
        Q6, etc.

12. Kt—B5   Kt—R5
13. Kt—K5!

Now White has an overwhelming game. The way in which
Steinitz has been able to achieve
such a sweeping advantage spot-
lights the general level of positional understanding at the time.
The player of that day usually
concerned himself with the attack
and had little use for positional
niceties. Such errors as Black
has committed here could never
occur in a master tournament
nowadays.

13. ....   Kt—B4
14. P—QB3   B × Kt

And now, without any real
need, Black exchanges off his
good Bishop instead of proceed-
ing in one way or another to
achieve the fianchetto of his Q-
Bishop.

15. R × B   Kt—B3
16. R—K1

Mainly in preparation for Kt—
Q3—K5.

16. ....   P—KR3

Preventing 17. B—KKt5 but
weakening the K-side.

17. Q—B3   Kt—Q4
18. B—Kt3

The Bishop is going to occupy
the QKt1—KR7 diagonal with-
out obstructing the manœuvre
Kt—Q3—K5. (If 18. B—Q3
Black replies 18. .... P—
QKt3!).

18. ....   P—QKt3
19. Kt—Q3   B—R3

At last the Bishop is free,
though still not well placed,
being unable to take part in the
defence of the K-side.

20. Kt—K5   R—B1
21. B—B2   Kt(B)—K2
22. Q—Kt3   K—R1
23. Q—R4

Threatening 24. B × P, etc.

23. ....   K—Kt1
24. Q—Kt3

24. B × P would not succeed
now because after 24. .... P ×
B; 25. Q × P, there would follow
25. .... Kt—B4.

24. ....   K—R1
25. Q—R3   Kt—Kt1

Black could also have returned
his King to Kt1, but it would
have made little difference.
White, with his Queen now out of
range of the black Knight, could
then have continued quietly reinforcing his attack: e.g. 26. R—
K4.

26. Q—R5   R—B2
27. B—Q2   Kt(4)—B3
28. Q—R3   Kt—Q4

Black can undertake absolutely
nothing.

29. P—QB4   Kt(4)—B3
30. QR—Q1

Indirect protection of the Q-
pawn.

30. ....   Q—K1
31. B—B4!

33

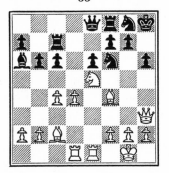

The decisive strengthening of White's position. He threatens to win the Exchange by 32. Kt—Kt6 ch, etc., and against this Black has no sufficient defence.

31. ....   R—B1
A few other possibilities:

A. 31. .... Q—Q1; 32. Kt—Kt4, R—Q2; 33. Kt × P, etc., with a winning attack.

B. 31. .... R—Kt2; 32. Q—R3! winning a piece.

C. 31. .... R—K2; 32. P—KKt4! with a winning attack; e.g.

> (1) 32. .... Kt—Q2; 33. Kt × QBP, etc.
>
> (2) 32. .... Kt—R2; 33. P—Kt5, P—Kt3; 34. Kt × KtP ch, P × Kt; 35. B—K5 ch, R—Kt2; 36. P × P, etc.

32. Q—R3!   B—Kt2
33. Q × P   B—R1
34. Q × KtP   P—Kt4
35. B—KKt3   Kt—Q2
36. Q—Kt3   P—KB4
37. P—B3   K—Kt2
38. P—B5   Kt(2)—B3
39. Kt—B4!   Resigns.

GAME 18

Here we see a new-style game, in which Steinitz demonstrates that his central majority carries more weight than that of his opponent on the Q-side.

White: J. H. ZUKERTORT   Black: W. STEINITZ
New Orleans, 1886.   *Queen's Gambit*

1. P—Q4   P—Q4
2. P—QB4   P—K3
3. Kt—QB3   Kt—KB3
4. B—Kt5   B—K2
5. Kt—B3   0—0
6. P—B5

White makes it his business to prevent the liberation of the black Q-Bishop. He is quite correct in feeling that the development of this piece is the main problem of the variation and he therefore deems it proper to undertake direct action.

But this conclusion is not justified. The sequel shows that the position was not yet ripe for this definite commitment which indeed rather facilitates the mobilization of Black's Q-Bishop. White would have done better to attend to his own development by 6. P—K3.

6. ....   P—QKt3!
A well-conceived counter action.

7. P—QKt4

Practically forced. It is clear that 7. P × P, RP × P would improve Black's prospects in several important ways: gain of tempo (since White's P—B5 and P × P were wasted moves); opportunity to play P—QB4 himself; strengthening of the centre; open QR-file; and development of the Q-Bishop via Kt2 or R3.

7. ....   P × P
8. QP × P

Again virtually forced. After 8. KtP × P there follows 8. .... B—R3! with the following difficulties for White:

A. 9. P—K3, B × B!, etc. White loses the K-side castling option and moreover trades his good Bishop for Black's bad one.

B. 9. P—Kt3. This is time-consuming and does not really provide much scope for the K-Bishop. The game might continue: 9. .... Kt—K5; 10. B × B, Q × B; 11. Kt × Kt, P × Kt; and then

  (1) 12. Kt—K5, P—KB3; 13. Kt—Kt4, P—K4; 14. P × P, Q × BP; with advantage to Black.

  (2) 12. Kt—Q2, P—B4; followed soon by P—K4 with very good play for Black.

8. ....   P—QR4

Now begins the struggle between the two majorities—Black's in the centre and White's on the Q-side. The text move is an important preparation for the advance of Black's centre pawns.

9. P—QR3

Forced, of course.

9. ....   P—Q5!

Thanks to Black's previous move this pawn cannot be taken: 10. Kt × P? P × P; etc. Or 10. Q × P? Q × Q; 11. Kt × Q, P × P; etc.

10. B × Kt

Either making 11. Kt—K4 playable or else forcing a slight weakening of the black K-side.

10. ....   P × B

This is better than 10. .... B × B. Under present circumstances the move chosen by Black is to be regarded more as a strengthening of the centre than a weakening of the K-side.

11. Kt—QR4

11. Kt—K4 would now be unfavourable because of the reply 11. .... P—B4.

11. ....   P—K4

Consequent play. It is now evident that White's plan has completely broken down, for the black Q-Bishop is fully liberated and White is suffering from retarded development.

There was another good continuation in 11. .... P × P; 12. P × P, Kt—B3; 13. P—Kt5, Kt—Kt5; 14. R—B1, Q—Q4, etc.

12. P—Kt5

With the powerful threat of 13. P—B6, which would imprison the black Q-Knight and thereby the Q-Rook as well.

12. ....   B—K3?

Steinitz underestimates the danger. 12. .... Q—Q4 was the proper move, with 12. ....

P—B3 and 12. .... Kt—Q2 also worth consideration.

13. P—Kt3?

White fails to make use of the opportunity which presents itself. By 13. P—B6! he might, it is true, have lost a pawn but would have gained a clear advantage:

A. 13. .... Q—Q4; 14. P—K3, P×P;

(1) 15. P×P? This fails against 15. .... Q×Q ch followed by 16. .... B—Kt6 (ch).

(2) 15. Q×Q! P×P ch; 16. K×P, B×Q; 17. Kt—B3 and White dominates the game.

B. 13. .... B—B5; 14. P—K4, P—Q6; 15. Kt—B3, P—R5; 16. Q—B1, R—R4; 17. R—QKt1, B—B4; 18. Kt—Q2, B—K3; 19. Kt×P, and again White dominates. Black's best continuation would be 19. .... B×P ch.

13. ....   P—B3

Putting an end, once for all, to any possibility of P—B6.

14. P×P

Or 14. P—Kt6, Q—Q4; 15. R—B1, Kt—Q2; 16. Q—B2, Q—Kt6, etc., with advantage to Black.

14. ....   Kt×P
15. B—Kt2   R—Kt1

Threatening 16. .... B—Kt6.

16. Q—B1   P—Q6!

Excellent. Black asserts his superior development.

17. P—K3

There is no reasonable alterna-tive, for White cannot allow the black Knight to go to Q5. After 17. P×P, Q×P; the white King, unable to castle, would be exposed to a destructive attack.

17. ....   P—K5
18. Kt—Q2   P—B4
19. 0—0   R—K1!

34

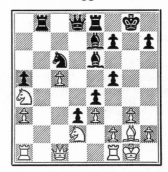

It is clear that Black now has an overwhelming position. His massive pawn centre has driven deep into enemy territory, while all that remains of the white Q-side majority is a blockaded isolated passed pawn which is more of a weakness to White than a danger to Black.

White nevertheless still has one important resource which consists of P—KB3 and/or P—KKt4, breaking up the black centre and putting the black King in danger. Black's fine move rebuts this line of play in advance. His idea is to play B—B3 with gain of tempo, and then by B—Q4 to put two more defences on his K-pawn.

20. P—B3

Against this immediate attack Black has yet another arrow to his bow.

20. ....   Kt—Q5!

Threatening not only Kt—K7 ch but also Kt—B7 followed by Kt × KP. There is nothing for it but to take.

21. P × Kt   Q × P ch
22. K—R1   P—K6!

The point. After 22. .... Q × Kt on the other hand White would have replied 23. P × P, etc., attaining his object. The outcome of the game would then have been uncertain.

23. Kt—B3   B—B3!

Once again a stronger move than the immediate regain of the piece. Black's advanced centre

has now become a pair of united passed pawns and is worth more than a Rook.

24. Kt(2)—Kt1   P—Q7
25. Q—B2   B—Kt6
26. Q × BP   P—Q8(Q)
27. Kt × Q   B × Kt

This is stronger than Q × R.

28. Kt—B3   P—K7
29. QR × B

Or 29. KR × B, P × R(Q) ch; 30. R × Q, Q × Kt, etc.

29. ....   Q × Kt

Black has regained his piece and still has a whole Rook to come. White resigns.

GAME 19

Just as in No.18 Steinitz here engages in a tough struggle against an opponent who evidently intended to follow the fundamentals of position play but nevertheless sinned against them. The desire to attack got the upper hand over the intention to be objective and a few premature moves were made, whereupon Steinitz inexorably exacted the full penalty.

White: H. N. PILLSBURY   Black: W. STEINITZ

New York, 1894.   *Queen's Gambit Accepted*

1. P—Q4   P—Q4
2. P—QB4   P × P

Queen's Gambit Accepted.

3. Kt—KB3

Forestalling 3. .... P—K4.

3. ....   P—K3
4. P—K3   P—QB4

After 4. .... P—QKt4; 5. P—QR4, P—QB3; 6. P × P, P × P; 7. P—QKt3, White regains his pawn with a good game.

5. Kt—QB3   Kt—QB3
6. B × P   Kt—B3

7. 0—0   P × P
8. P × P   B—K2
9. B—B4

Steinitz has his favourite variation again and White makes the same mistake as in Game 15. (See note at move 11 of that game.)

9. ....   0—0
10. R—B1   Q—Kt3
11. Kt—QKt5

Introducing a nicely-planned operation which, however, seems to be premature. 11. Q—Q2 was the move (11. .... R—Q1; 12. B—K3). White would then have had a very reasonable game.

11. .... Kt—K1

Forced, the main threat being 12. B—B7, Q—R3; 13. Kt—Q6, etc.

12. R—K1	Kt—R4
13. B—Q3	B—Q2
14. Kt—B7	R—B1

After 14. .... Kt × Kt? 15. B × Kt the other Knight would be lost.

15. Kt—Q5! P × Kt
16. R × B

White has combined well and seems now to have some slight advantage, for the pawn position has become symmetrical and he has the two Bishops. The sequel will show, however, that the whole operation was premature.

16. .... Kt—KB3

35

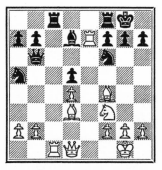

A further examination of the position leads to the surprising conclusion that it is in fact Black who has the better chances.

The momentum of White's attack is spent for the present and now it suddenly emerges that, thanks to several little threats, Black has the initiative. White's QKt-pawn is attacked; his Q-pawn can be besieged by B—Kt5 and Kt—QB3; finally the outlying Rook is in danger of being cut off by B—K3 and then captured by Kt—QB3. To parry all these threats White will at least have to relinquish his hard-earned advantage of the two Bishops.

17. Kt—Kt5

White goes ahead with his attacking policy; in the circumstances it is the best thing he can do. He threatens 18. Kt × RP, or 18. B × P ch, to be followed by 19. R × B; or even 18. R × B, to be followed by B × P ch and Q—R5.

Passive defence would have little chance of success here; e.g. 17. R—K2?, B—Kt5; 18. R(2)—B2, R × R; 19. R × R, B × Kt; 20. P × B, Kt—B3; and Black's game is excellent.

17. .... B—Kt5

This compels White to simplify whereas after, for instance, 17. .... P—KR3; White could continue 18. Kt—R7 with attacking chances.

18. B × P ch

Otherwise the Q-pawn falls (18. P—B3, Q × P ch; or 18. Q—Q2, R × R ch; 19. Q × R, Q × QP).

18.	Kt × B
19. Q × B	R × R ch
20. B × R	Kt—KB3
21. Q—Q1	Kt—B3
22. R—K1	Q × QP

Black has made important progress. He has forced White to exchange one of his Bishops and has won a centre pawn in exchange for a wing pawn. Since, moreover, the Q-pawn is now a passed pawn there is no doubt that Black's game is superior. The advantage, however, is not yet decisive.

23. Kt—B3!   Q—Kt3!

Well played on both sides. The struggle centres on the blockade square, White's Q4. After 23. .... Q × Q; 24. R × Q, R—K1; 25. B—K3, White's prospects are better, for the Q-pawn is stopped and might in the end turn out to be a weakness.

24. B—Kt5

Unable to control the blockade square White tries another tack—and correctly, for he cannot simply let Black play 24. .... P—Q5. The passed pawn would then be too dangerous.

24. ....   Q × KtP
25. R—K2?

After this move, which in fact amounts to a pawn sacrifice, White is definitely at a serious disadvantage. The proper play was 25. B × Kt, Q × B; 26. Q × P. It is true that the resulting position would still have contained one feature favouring Black, namely the Q-side majority; but this might not have yielded a win.

25. ....   Q—Kt4
26. B × Kt   P × B

Black has won a pawn and moreover he retains his strong passed pawn. These advantages count for more than the disadvantage of a weakened K-side.

27. R—Q2   R—Q1
28. Kt—R4

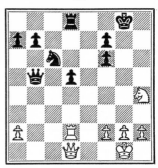

36

This further attempt to attack only accelerates the loss. By occupying the vital blockade square with 28. Kt—Q4! White could yet have put up a tough resistance.

28. ....   P—Q5!

The passed pawn is now too far advanced to be blockaded with any chance of success. The text move also gives Black the further advantage of a considerable superiority in terrain.

29. R—Q3   Kt—K4
30. R—QKt3   Q—B3
31. R—Kt3 ch   K—B1
32. Q—Q2

In order at least to get in a few checks.

32. ....   R—B1
33. Q—R6 ch   K—K2
34. Kt—B5 ch   K—Q2

The checks are exhausted and against the threat of 35. .... Q—B8 ch White is helpless.

35. P—KR4   Q—B8 ch
36. Q × Q   R × Q ch
37. K—R2   P—Q6

The win of a piece is now certain. White resigned.

GAME 20

A glorious yet tragic example—glorious in the consummate strategic manœuvring with which Steinitz first conducts a cool-headed defence and then secures a winning advantage; at the same time tragic in the elementary way in which he finally allows the win to slip through his fingers.

White: DR. EM. LASKER   Black: W. STEINITZ

Match, Moscow, 1896.   *Ruy Lopez*

1. P—K4	P—K4
2. Kt—KB3	Kt—QB3
3. B—Kt5	P—Q3

The simplest defence to the Lopez. Today's theory does not recommend it, since it allows White a great advantage in terrain. But methods of dealing with such general advantages were not common knowledge at the time. Direct attack was the order of the day and it is precisely these tactics which have little chance of success against the text-move.

For this reason Steinitz reaped quite a harvest of successes with 3. .... P—Q3; and the impression grew that this was indeed the best defence to the Ruy Lopez.

4. P—Q4	B—Q2
5. Kt—B3	KKt—K2

Black means to hold the centre (i.e. his K-pawn). From this point of view the move is logical but on the other hand it carries with it the great disadvantage of restricting Black's freedom of movement still more. Nor is 5. .... Kt—B3 very satisfactory, because of 6. B × Kt! B × B; 7. Q—Q3, which just about forces 7. .... P × P; and then White gets a splendid game by 8. Kt × P followed by B—Kt5 and 0—0—0.

6. B—Kt5

This is grist to Black's mill. White has more promising moves in 6. B—QB4 and 6. P × P, as played in other games between these two opponents (in the 1894 match and in the St. Petersburg Quadrangular Tournament of 1895/6).

6. ....   P—B3

Thus the K-pawn is given an extra defence, and with gain of tempo.

7. B—K3   Kt—B1

A well-considered move. Black vacates his K2 for the Bishop and at the same time sees to it that White shall not be able to occupy the nice diagonal from his QKt3 to KKt8 (8. B—QB4, Kt—Kt3; 9. B—Kt3, Kt—R4; and the Bishop will be eliminated).

8. Kt—K2

White intends to open a line of retreat for his K-Bishop. His policy is also, as far as possible, to avoid exchanges.

A simpler and equally good continuation would have been to occupy the central square Q5; e.g. 8. Kt—Q5, Kt—Kt3; 9. P × P! and White holds the initiative:

A. 9. .... BP × P; 10. B—Kt5, etc.

B. 9. .... Kt × Kt; 10. P × Kt, Kt × P; 11. B × B ch, Q × B; 12. Kt—Q4!, etc.

C. 9. .... QP × P; 10. Q—K2, etc.

| 8. .... | B—K2 |
| 9. P—B3 | O—O |

37

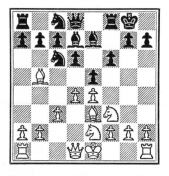

Black's position is solid and devoid of any weakness. Nevertheless, he is in for an arduous game on account of his limited freedom of movement.

White may therefore be said to have a slight advantage for his position is also intact. Both sides, however, will have to manœuvre with great care, White aiming to create attacking chances without taking risks, and Black trying to increase his freedom of movement.

10. B—Q3	Kt—Kt3
11. Kt—Kt3	K—R1
12. O—O	Q—K1
13. R—B1

Presumably intending 14. P—B4 and 15. P—Q5. For any other plan the Rook would not be well placed on QB1.

| 13. .... | Kt—Q1 |
| 14. R—K1 |

White changes plan, having evidently decided that neither 14. P—B4 nor 14. P—Q5 would achieve much.

| 14. .... | P—QB4 |

Black has manœuvred with great singleness of purpose. With this move he tries to force the white Q-pawn to do something, so as to clarify the situation in the centre.

15. Kt—Q2

Thus Black is kept in the dark about White's future plans—good tactics, in principle. The side with the less freedom always finds it very awkward to be faced with several dangers at once. Here he has to watch the possibilities of White's P—Q5, P × BP or P—KB4, steering the game into three quite different channels.

All the same White's move is not altogether satisfactory, for it allows Black to gain ground on the Q-side. A more obvious idea would have been to play 15. P × BP and then try to make something out of the weak square at Black's Q4. (Compare White's Q4 in Diagram 19.) However, this plan also would have been unlikely to succeed, for its realization would have required a wholesale time-consuming re-grouping of the white pieces.

No, White's idea of not showing his colours for the moment was the correct one; but a better way of carrying it out would have been 15. P—Kt3 and only then 16. Kt—Q2.

| 15. .... | Kt—R5! |

This is a strong move, and White should not have permitted it.

16. R—B2

If 16. P—Kt3? there are two possibilities:

A. 16. .... Kt—Kt7; 17. Q—B2, Kt × B; 18. Q × Kt. This would suit White very well; but

B. 16. .... Kt × P! 17. R × Kt, BP × P; 18. B × P, P × B would be to Black's advantage.

16. ....   P—QKt4!
17. P—KB4   Kt—K3!

With these last three moves Black has obtained fine counterplay. White is now forced to release the tension in the centre and moreover he must do it by closing the game, his Rooks being badly placed for opening either the Q-file or the KB-file.

18. P—B5   Kt—Q1
19. P—Q5

Thus both sides have established local territorial advantage —White on the K-side and Black on the Q-side. Heavy fighting is now in the offing, with attack and counterattack. Under present circumstances neither side can settle for a passive policy.

19. ....   Kt—Kt2
20. Kt—B3   P—B5
21. B—K2   B—Q1

In view of the pawn position this Bishop must be considered bad on the K-side but good on the Q-side; with the black Q-Bishop it is just the reverse. Steinitz therefore transfers his K-Bishop to the Q-side (B—Kt3) meanwhile holding his Q-Bishop in readiness for a sortie on the K-side via K1.

22. Kt—R4!

A powerful attacking move,

threatening to bring a decision at once by 23. B—R5, Q—K2; 24. Kt—Kt6 ch!, P × Kt; 25. B × P, with mate to follow by 26. Q—R5 ch, etc.

22. ....   P—Kt3

Forced.

23. B—Kt4

Introducing a new threat: 24. P × P, P × P; 25. B × B, Q × B; 26. Kt × P ch. White is certainly making adroit use of his K-side chances, but not without making some concessions. This last move has weakened his **Q3** and Black proceeds to take advantage right away.

23. ....   P—Kt4

It stands to reason that Black must keep the K-side closed if it is in any way possible.

24. Kt—B3   Kt(2)—B4

Here comes a Knight to occupy his **Q6**, and White can do nothing about it.

25. P—R4

The crisis approaches. White forces an opening on the K-side and concentrates all his forces for the attack, even at the cost of a pawn on the other wing.

25. ....   P × P
26. Kt × P   Kt—Q6
27. R—KB1!

By 27. R(1)—K2 White would obstruct his own Queen, and still not secure the Q-side. The continuation would be 27. .... Kt(6) × P; 28. R × Kt, Kt × P; followed by 29. .... Kt × R ch with fine play for Black.

27.	Kt(5) × KtP
28. Q—B3	B—Kt3
29. K—R2	R—KKt1
30. B—R6	Q—K2
31. Kt—R5	

White has an extremely dangerous attack.

| 31. .... | B—K1 |

See the note to 21. .... B—Q1. Black is playing a cool-headed defence. With the text move he takes precautions against a possible Kt—Kt6 ch and gives himself the alternative option of destroying the other Knight if necessary.

| 32. Q—R3 | Kt—R5 |

38

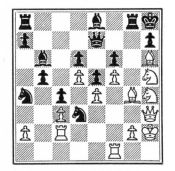

A position decidedly out of the ordinary. Nearly all the white pieces are lined up on the KR-file—except the very ones which ought to be there, namely the Rooks: not a very pretty arrangement. Nevertheless White's attack is strong, for Black has not many pieces available for defensive purposes. This state of affairs cannot last very long, for Black is better off than White in the matter of reinforcements owing to his material advantage.

The moment of crisis is therefore already at hand. Everything now depends on whether White can find a winning—or at least a saving—line in the next few moves.

33. B—B3

White hesitates—and from the practical point of view he is certainly wrong to do so. He tries to strengthen his position but all he achieves is a hopelessly lost game. 33. Kt—Kt6 ch, though not altogether convincing, would have brought about great complications and therefore offered fair chances of saving the situation: e.g.

A. 33. .... P × Kt?; 34. Kt × P!, R—Kt2; 35. B × R ch, K × B; 36. Q—R7 ch, K × Kt; 37. P × P ch, Kt—B5; 38. Q—R4 ch and White wins the Queen.

B. 33. .... B × Kt!; 34. P × B, R × P;
 (1) 35. R × P?, R × R; 36. B—Kt5,
  (*a*) 36. .... QR—KB1; 37. Kt × R, R × Kt; 38. B—B5, K—Kt1; 39. Q—R4!, B—Q1; 40. B × R, Q × B; 41. Q × P ch and White has drawing chances.
  (*b*) 36. .... Kt—B5!; 37. B × R ch, Q × B; 38. Kt × Q, Kt × Q, etc., with a won endgame for Black.
 (2) 35. Kt × P!, R × Kt; 36. B—Kt5,
  (*a*) 36. .... Kt—B5?; 37. Q—R4, QR—KB1; 38. P—Kt3, with advantage to White.
  (*b*) 36. .... R × R; 37. B × Q, B—Kt8 ch;

(i) 38. K—Kt3? This gives Black a winning attack; e.g. 38. .... R—KKt1!; 39. Q—R4, R—Kt3; 40. B—Kt5, Kt(5)—B4; 41. B—B5, R(8) × B; 42. P × R, R × B ch, etc.

(ii) 38. K—R1! and Black must be content with perpetual check.

(c) 36. .... QR—KB1; If Black wants to play for a win this is the variation he must choose, although it is anything but clear. There would follow 37. R × R, R × R; 38. B—B5, which runs into variation B(1) (a) but by a forced sequence.

33.	Kt(5)—B4
34. R—K2	Kt—Q2
35. P—Kt3	

Already White has to be thinking of his own defence. He prepares for Kt—Kt2—K3. Possibly he also reckons on returning to the attack later on by K—Kt2 and R—KR1, but this hope is never fulfilled.

35.	P—R4
36. Kt—Kt2	P—Kt5
37. Kt—K3	R—QB1
38. Kt—Q1	P × P

Black's game is won; his Q-side advantage must be decisive. The text is good enough, though 38. .... P—Kt6 or 38. .... Kt(2)—B4 would have been still stronger.

39. Kt(1) × P	B—Q5
40. B—Q2	Kt(2)—B4
41. Q—R4	B(1) × Kt
42. B × B	R—Kt1
43. Kt—Q1	Kt—R5

The passed QB-pawn guarantees the win. There is no need, therefore, for Black to spend time holding on to his extra pawn.

44. B × P	R—R1
45. B—Q2	P—B6
46. B × P!	

A smart resource; White loses the Exchange but can still put up a resistance. After any other move Black would have won quickly by KR—QB1 followed by P—B7.

46.	Kt × B
47. Kt × Kt	B × Kt
48. R—B3	Kt—B8
49. R—QB2	Kt × P
50. R(3) × B	Kt × R
51. R × Kt	

The immediate danger is averted now that Black has no passed pawn.

| 51. .... | KR—QB1 |

The second little inexactitude in the winning process. 51. .... R—Kt4 would have been better calculated to deprive White of any counter-chances.

| 52. R—Kt3 | R—R7 ch |
| 53. K—R3 | R(7)—QB7 |

And here it would have been stronger to play 53. .... R—R8, forcing the white Bishop back to KB3. But the win is still safe.

| 54. R—Kt6 |

The last chance; White has a little pleasantry in mind.

| 54. .... | R(7)—B6 |
| 55. B—Kt6 | |

This threatens 56. R × P, and gives Black the opportunity to make a serious blunder.

55. ....   R—Q1??

39

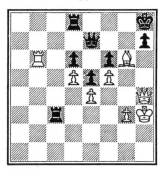

At the very last moment Steinitz allows himself to be robbed of his win. What a pity, for a game played in such lordly style. After 55. .... R(6)—B2, giving the R-pawn an extra protection, White would have finally come to the end of his resources.

56. R—Kt7!
Pretty, though obvious enough. White now forces perpetual check.

56. ....   Q × R
Or 56. .... R—B2; 57. R × R, Q × R; 58. Q × BP ch, K—Kt1; 59. B—B7 ch, etc.

57. Q × BP ch   Q—Kt2
If 57. .... K—Kt1 there follows 58. Q × R ch, K—Kt2; 59. B—R5, etc.

58. Q × R ch   Q—Kt1
59. Q—B6 ch
Draw.

GAME 21

In this game we see Steinitz putting the two Bishops to excellent use. He obtains them as early as the fifth move and then proceeds, step by step, to make their influence felt. The course of the game runs parallel to No. 20. After establishing a won position by exemplary strategy Steinitz lets it slip, and wins in the end only thanks to a blunder by his opponent.

White: G. R. NEUMANN   Black: W. STEINITZ
Baden-Baden, 1870. *Dutch Defence*

1. P—Q4   P—KB4
The Dutch Defence.

2. P—K4
This variation is known as the Staunton Gambit.

2. ....   P × P
3. Kt—QB3   Kt—KB3
Not 3. .... P—Q4? because of 4. Q—R5 ch and 5. Q × QP.

4. B—KKt5   P—B3

Again not 4. .... P—Q4? because of 5. B × Kt followed by Q—R5 ch and Q × QP. But the text move also entails difficulties. Nowadays 4. .... P—KKt3 is reckoned best.

5. B × Kt
Illogical and weak. 5. P—B3! was the move here.

Instinctively one asks how White could refrain from such a move as 5. P—B3 in a period when gambits were so much in vogue. The explanation is probably to be sought in the lack of general principles. Certain gambits were very well known, especially the K-Gambit and the Evans; but to judge when gambit tactics would be justified in other openings was another matter.

5.	KP × B
6. Kt × P	

The pawn is regained but Black has the two Bishops, and as White has no sort of compensation this constitutes some slight advantage to Black.

6.	P—Q4

Theory holds that 6. .... Q—Kt3 is even stronger, chiefly because the line 7. Q—K2, Q × KtP! works out in Black's favour.

7. Kt—Kt3	Q—Kt3
8. Q—K2 ch	K—B2!

Economic defence. The King is perfectly safe here, and needs no help; and there is an immediate threat of 9. .... B—Kt5 ch and 10. .... R—K1.

9. O—O—O	Kt—R3
10. Q—B3	P—Kt3

To prevent 11. Kt—B5, but also with an ulterior motive which will shortly appear.

11. B—Q3

Now White's remaining Bishop will soon be exchanged for a Knight; but other moves would involve just as much difficulty. White is ill at ease; from the dynamic point of view his development leaves much to be desired.

11.	Kt—Kt5
12. K—Kt1	P—KR4!

40

10. .... P—Kt3 was played with this powerful advance in mind. It threatens to win the Exchange by 13. .... B—Kt5, but its real intention is to drive away the Knight which stands at Kt3 and thus ensure the development of the Q-Bishop to KB4.

This is the advantage of Bishops over Knights: the Bishops operate at long range and are therefore only to a slight extent vulnerable to attack by pawns.

Steinitz here shows us how the two Bishops come into their own: the Knights are driven back by the pawns so that they cannot command any vital points in enemy territory. The Bishops meanwhile continue to exert their influence, so that whoever has the Bishops also has the initiative.

13. P—KR3

White has nothing better. If, for instance, 13. B—K2 there follows 13. .... P—R5; 14. Kt—B1, P—R6! with great advantage to Black. (After 15. Kt × P, B—KB4 Black answers 16. R—B1 by 16. .... R × Kt! and 16. B—Q3 by 16. .... Kt × B; 17. P × Kt, B × Kt; 18. P × B,

Q × QP; leaving White with a hopelessly wrecked pawn position.

13.	....	P—R5
14.	Kt(3)—K2	Kt × B
15.	R × Kt	B—KB4

Having repulsed the Knight and exchanged the Bishop, Black now occupies the fine square KB4 with his Bishop.

16.	R—Kt3	Q—B2
17.	Kt—B4	B—K5

This achieves nothing but also spoils nothing. Perhaps White will play 18. Q—K3? whereupon Black wins quickly with 18. .... B—R3.

18.	Q—Kt4	B—KB4

No success achieved, but no harm done. The white Queen must return to B3 and the Black is exactly where he was two moves ago. He could force a draw by repetition but of course does no such thing.

Situations like this, where both sides can make a few moves very quickly, are useful when playing with clocks, both sides conserving their time. It is certainly some advantage to be the one who is in a position to force such a repetition.

19.	Q—B3	B—Q3
20.	Kt(1)—K2	P—R4

An advance similar to that on the 12th move. This time he drives a Rook instead of a Knight, but the object is the same—to deprive the Knights of squares.

The player with the two Bishops generally risks nothing by pushing on his pawns, provided that by so doing he does not create weak squares, especially in the central zone. Should this happen the game might swing the other way, for Knights are pre-eminently suited for occupying and exploiting weak squares.

The advance of the two black wing pawns is characteristic of this type of game.

21.	R—Kt1	P—R5
22.	R—K3	QR—K1

As far as possible the Bishop player must avoid fixing his own pawns for this would make it difficult to open the game. It follows that 22. .... P—R6; 23. P—QKt3 would have eased White's task.

23.	P—KKt3	B—K5
24.	Q—Kt4	B—KB4

Apparently this is played only to gain time. (See note to move 18.)

25. R × R

White makes this capture in the faint hope that Black may take the Queen for two Rooks. After 25. Q—B3, R × R; 26. Q × R, R—K1; 27. Q—KB3 (27. Q—QB3?, P—KKt4!) we should have exactly the same position as that which arises in the actual game after White's 26th move.

25.	....	R × R!
26.	Q—B3	Q—R4

Threatening Q—Q7.

27.	K—B1	Q—R3

Now the threat is Q—B5, winning the QR-pawn or the QB-pawn or the Q-pawn.

28. Kt—B3   P—QKt4

Threatening 29. .... P—Kt5 and 30. .... Q—B5. One by one Black has established a series of advantages and now he considers the time is ripe to go over to the attack. With the text move he accepts the creation of a weak square at his QB4, in the belief that the position of the white pieces will not allow them to take advantage of the weakness within a reasonable time.

Such a policy—the acceptance of one sort of weakness in order to gain some other sort of advantage—is frequently necessary; but it requires an exact evaluation of the chances. In the present case Black has judged well: the hole at his QB4 does indeed play a part, but only a subordinate one.

29. P—KKt4   B—QB1
30. Kt—Q1   P—Kt5
31. Kt—K3   P—Kt6!

41

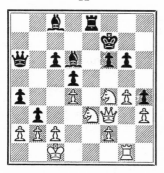

White has prevented the dangerous Q—B5 but now his K-position will be broken up.

32. P—R3

Forced. After any other move the black attack would be irresistible.

32. ....   P×P

Black's weakness at QB4 is now amply counter-balanced by that at White's QKt3.

33. P—Kt5   P—KB4

White may have been hoping to make something out of the artificial isolation of Black's KR-pawn. His own KR-pawn, however, is a compensating weakness.

34. Kt×QBP   Q—B5
35. Kt—Kt2   R—K7
36. Kt—K1

After 36. Kt—K3 Black would retire Q—Kt4, leaving the Knight exposed to attack by P—B5.

36. ....   P—B5

It begins to look as though the white position will collapse at any moment, but it is not as bad as all that.

37. K—Q1   R—K5
38. Kt—Kt2   Q—Kt6

Now White cannot exchange Queens without losing his Q-pawn.

39. Q—B3   Q×Q
40. P×Q

White has defended so tenaciously that Black now sees no chance of forcing a win by direct attack. He therefore goes into the endgame, and under very favourable circumstances.

40. ....   B×KRP
41. P—B3

The immediate capture on R4 would be fatal: 41. .... P—B6!;

Kt × BP, B—KKt5; **43.** Kt—
K1, R × Kt ch, etc.

41.	R—K1
42. Kt × RP	R—KR1
43. Kt—Kt2	R—R4
44. Kt(Kt2)—K1	B—KB4

Black obviously dominates;
not only has he the two Bishops
but also the better Rook position.

| **45.** Kt—Kt4 | B—Q2 |
| | Forced. |

46. R—Kt2

Not **46.** Kt(1)—Q3 at once
because after **46.** .... R—R7!
White's game would rapidly become hopeless with a black Rook
commanding his second rank.

| **46.** .... | K—K3 |

Now Black threatens to win
the white Kt-pawn; but White
still finds a way of saving it.

| **47.** Kt(1)—Q3 | K—B4 |
| **48.** Kt—Kt2! | |

This threat against the QR-
pawn compels Black to leave the
KKt-pawn alone and instead
go after the white R-pawn,
which would otherwise become
very menacing.

48.	R—R8 ch!
49. K—B2	R—R8
50. Kt × RP	R × P
51. Kt—B5	

White scores at least a moral
success by occupying the weak
square at Black's QB4.

| **51.** .... | B × Kt! |

The beginning of a winning
liquidation. The Bishop-pair as
such has done its work, and now
the superior placing of Black's

King and Rook must bring the
decision.

| **52.** P × B | |

42

| **52.** .... | P—Q5! |

This was Black's point in
making the preceding capture.
The indirect exchange of Black's
Q-pawn for White's KB-pawn
makes the black KB-pawn into a
passed pawn. The decisive factor is the fact that it can advance,
escorted by the King.

| **53.** P × P | R × P |
| **54.** P—Q5 | |

The last chance. Otherwise
Black plays **54.** .... K—K5
with an easy win.

| **54.** .... | R—KKt6 |

Stronger than **54.** .... P × P;
which would allow White to win
an important tempo with **55.** P—
B6.

| **55.** R—B2 | P—B6 |
| **56.** P × P | B—K3 |

Black threatens an immediate
decision by **57.** .... R—Kt7.
White's doubled passed pawns
meanwhile are not particularly
dangerous.

57. K—Q2   K—K5

Now the black threat is **58. .... R × P;** and **59. ....
R × P;** winning with ease.

58. R—B1   R—Kt7 ch

58. .... R × P would not be
so good now, because of **59. R—
K1 ch, K—B4; 60. P—B7.**

59. K—B3   R—K7
60. P—B7   R—K6 ch

Another repetition to gain
time. The winning move was
60. .... P—B7.

61. K—Q2   R—K7 ch
62. K—Q1

White sees the win (**62. K—
B3, P—B7!**) and therefore varies
with his King.

62. ....   B—Kt6 ch
63. K—B1   B—K3

The same old game, and again
White is a spoilsport. The win
which he spots this time is
64. K—Q1, B—Kt5!

64. Kt—B2   B—B1
65. K—Q1   B—Kt5

Now Black is on the right
track.

66. P—B6   K—B5
67. Kt—Q4   R—K1
68. K—Q2   R—QB1?

With this tactical error Black
throws away the win. After the
simple **68. .... K—Kt6** it
would have been all over, for the
KB-pawn would at least have
cost the Knight.

69. K—Q3   K—Kt6

Black realizes that he has
blundered. If **69. .... R × P,**

as intended, White can force the
draw by **70. R × P ch, B × R;
71. Kt—K6 ch** and **72. Kt × R.**

The mistake cannot be remed-
ied. The lost time and the
abandoned K-file will be avenged.

70. R—Kt1 ch   K—B5

After **70. .... K—R6; 71. K—
K3!** the draw would be still
easier for White.

71. R—KB1   K—Kt6
72. R—Kt1 ch   K—B5
73. R—KB1   R—K1

There is no hope of achieving
anything except by reoccupying
the K-file.

74. K—B4

The saving plan: the white
King advances to support his
passed pawn.

74. ....   K—Kt6
75. Kt × P   B × Kt
76. R × B ch   K × R
77. K—Q5

Correct; either **77. K—Kt5** or
77. K—B5 would have been refuted easily by **77. .... K—K5;
78. K—Kt6, K—Q4; 79. K—
Kt7, K—Q3; 80. P—B8(Q), R ×
Q; 81. K × R, K × P,** etc.

77. ....   R—QR1!

The best chance. At least the
white King will not reach Q7
with gain of tempo.

78. K—K5!

The only move to draw. After
78. K—Q6?, K—K5 etc., Black
would win. (See note to **77. K—
Q5.**)

78. ....   K—K6!

After other King moves, e.g. 78. .... K—Kt5? it would be White who would win—by 79. K—Q6! Black must see to it that he can answer K—Q6 with K—K5!

79. K—B6
The last finesse. White cannot force his B-pawns in but now he wins the Kt-pawn, after which his own Kt-pawn secures the draw.

79.	R—QB1
80. K × P	K—B5
81. K—B6	R × P
82. P—Kt6	R × P ch
83. K—B7	K—B4
84. P—Kt7	R—B2 ch
85. K—B8	K—B3!
	Threatening mate.

86. P—Kt8(Kt) ch!
The only way. By the skin of his teeth White achieves a theoretical draw.

86.	K—K3
87. Kt—R6	R—KR2

43

There is no point in any further attempt to win. In any master tournament today this position would be abandoned as a draw without more ado.

88. Kt—Kt4?
An elementary blunder which quickly leads to the loss of the Knight. Apparently the rule that in such positions the Knight should always stay close to the King was little known—even among the top players. 88. Kt—Kt8—an obvious move to modern eyes—would have drawn comfortably; e.g. 88. .... R—B2 ch; 89. K—K8, and now:

A. 89. .... R—QR2; 90. K—B8, etc.

B. 89. .... R—B8; 90. Kt—R6
  (1) 90. .... R—KKt8;
    91. K—B8, etc.
  (2) 90. .... R—KR8;
    91. Kt—Kt8, etc.

88.	R—R5

89. Kt—K3
After 89. Kt—B2 the Knight is lost at once by R—B5 ch.

89.	R—K5

90. Kt—Q1
The Knight is lost, however, he plays:

A. 90. Kt—B1, R—B5 ch, etc.

B. 90. Kt—Kt2, K—B3; 91. K—Kt8, R—Kt5 ch, etc.

C. 90. Kt—B2, K—Q4; 91. Kt—R3, K—B4; 92. Kt—Kt1, K—Kt5; 93. Kt—Q2, R—K7; followed by 94. .... R—KB7 (ch), etc., or 94. .... R—Kt7.

90.	R—B5 ch
91. K—Kt7	R—B6
92. K—Kt6	K—K4

93. K—Kt5   K—Q5
94. K—Kt4

The white King arrives too late to release the Knight.

94. ....   R—B8
95. Kt—Kt2   R—QKt8
96. Kt—R4   R—Kt5

White resigns, for the Knight is checkmated! An instructive game from beginning to end.

44

☆ 6 ☆

TECHNIQUE AND ROUTINE
The Virtuosi (1900–1914)

THE REIGN of Steinitz was followed by a kind of lull in the development of chess.   Everyone was busy working out and refining the new ideas and for the time there seemed to be no need of anything really fresh.   Only when old methods are wearing thin does the need for new thinking arise.   For the moment there was abundance of novelty still barely comprehended.

The difference in outlook between Steinitz and his contemporaries had produced an unnaturally wide division between attacking play and position play; it was time now to bridge the gap.   This task was accomplished by the next generation—a generation of masters uncommonly rich in talent.

These masters we call the virtuosi, for they generally sought only for perfect application of principles already known.   They acknowledged Steinitz as their teacher without in any way regarding him as their ideal.   They were not extremists; they exhibited no prejudices.   They readily accepted what was good wherever they could make use of it.   Sifting and refining all the time they strove to reconcile the extremes—attacking play with position play; theory with practice; the desirable with the possible.   Compared with their predecessors the virtuosi shone primarily in their fine technique in every phase of the game—even in the domain of combination.   They improved and extended the Steinitz principles with countless little rules, and were also able to extract important lessons from those who had left no teaching behind them but only sparkling games—particularly Morphy and Anderssen.

Thus the virtuosi attained to an uncommonly good grasp of the requirements of the game.   They raised the general standard of play considerably and many of them are to be ranked among the greatest players in the history of chess.

It is difficult to know where to begin when one is dealing with a whole generation.   We have selected 1900, the year when Steinitz died, but some of these masters whom we term the virtuosi had been prominent since the 1880s. The finish of the era however can be pin-pointed precisely, for it was terminated by an elemental upheaval—the outbreak of the 1914–18 war.

During the time of the virtuosi chess style in general underwent a gradual modification. With technique as its starting point it drifted towards routine. At times there was an exaggerated trust in science; players tended all too willingly to hold on to the leading-strings of calculation. The spirit of enterprise which had marked the attacks of Anderssen and Morphy, which characterized the defensive operations of Steinitz, and which also animated the first of the virtuosi, eventually spent itself. In the final years before 1914 games occurred between front-rank masters in which only routine and no fighting spirit at all could be descried. They were short and boringly correct draws.

Up to now we have named no names, lest we should give the wrong impression that these developments were due to any one individual. The fact that they were extraordinarily strong players is beside the point. Not one of them can be considered as the founder of a new style—least of all the world champion, Lasker, for his ascendancy arose mainly from his rare skill in the handling of complicated positions, an art which cannot be taught. Tarrasch admittedly appeared in the rôle of teacher and established many rules; but he was concerned with detail and interpretation, amplifying and clarifying the teaching of Steinitz.

And so we could go on, reciting a series of resounding names; but we shall confine ourselves in this chapter to Pillsbury and Marshall, the heroes of combination, Maróczy and Rubinstein, the great strategists and endgame experts, and above all Capablanca, the perfectionist.

GAME 22

Steinitz, just like the combinative players who opposed him, had a risky style. They, on the one hand, cared less about theoretical disadvantages than about practical opportunities; Steinitz, on the other hand, clung to theoretical advantages, undeterred by any practical difficulties. Midway between these two extreme points of view stands Siegbert Tarrasch (1862–1934) the first great virtuoso. By nature he was very cautious, and he had no particular bent for combination; but the one thing which he had grasped better than any of his predecessors was the importance of rapid, economical development of his forces—of course without any sacrifices. He followed the general lines of Steinitz but attached much more value to the activity of the pieces. He liked to make a point of depriving his opponent of all good moves, and referred to his own methods as the 'stalemating style'. For a considerable time Tarrasch was the best technician in the world. He was extraordinarily successful also as a teacher, for he had the knack of popularizing the fundamentals of position play. This game gives a good idea of the views and capabilities of Tarrasch.

White: S. TARRASCH   Black: W. STEINITZ

Nuremberg, 1896.   *Ruy Lopez*

1. P—K4	P—K4
2. Kt—KB3	Kt—QB3
3. B—Kt5	P—B3

Tarrasch admitted that this move is not nearly as bad as it seems. This, however, implied his own firm conviction that the square KB3 should obviously be reserved for the K-Knight.

4. 0—0	KKt—K2
5. P—Q4	Kt—Kt3
6. P—QR3	

This is played in order to install the K-Bishop on the diagonal QR2—KKt8 and to safeguard it from exchange. When playing White Tarrasch considered that the K-Bishop—the attacking Bishop as he called it—was the strongest of all his minor pieces.

6.	B—K2
7. B—QB4	P—Q3
8. P—R3	

Depriving the black Q-Bishop of its best square.

8.	B—Q2
9. Kt—B3	Q—B1
10. K—R2	

The Bishop sacrifice at White's KR3 would certainly not have given a sufficient attack, yet Tarrasch prevents it, for he is of a more practical turn of mind than Steinitz: in a defensive position it is easy to make a slip.

10.	Kt—Q1

Steinitz habitually manœuvred in this fashion. See Game 20.

11. Kt—Q5	

Tarrasch explains that he made this move chiefly in order to provoke Black to P—QB3, which in this position would be a slight weakening.

11.	B—B1

Typical Steinitz: he gives away nothing at all, preferring rather to accept the greatest difficulty over his own development. 11. .... Kt—K3, giving up the Bishop-pair, would have involved far less trouble.

12. B—K3	Kt—K3
13. Kt—Kt1	

A move which aims to deny Black any shadow of initiative, such as he might get by establishing a Knight at KB5.

13.	P—B3

Not good; but a decent move for Black is already difficult to find.

14. Kt—QB3	B—K2

14. .... Kt(K3)—B5 would have revealed the point of 13. Kt—Kt1, thus: 15. B × Kt, Kt × B; 16. P—KKt3! and now 16. .... Kt × P? would cost a

piece by 17. Kt × Kt, B × Kt; 18. Q—R5 ch, etc.

15. KKt—K2
Preparing 16. P—B4

15. .... Q—B2
Crossing White's intention.

16. P—Q5
And not 16. P—B4? for after 16. .... Kt(K3) × BP; 17. Kt × Kt, Kt × Kt; 18. B × Kt, P × B Black has won a pawn, White being unable to capture with the Rook without losing a piece by 19. .... P—Q4!

16. .... Kt—Q1
17. Kt—Kt3 Kt—B2
18. Kt—B5
White's position is now overwhelming.

18. .... B—KB1

45

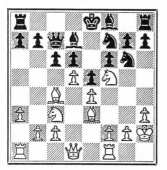

This fresh retreat is decidedly mistaken, but there was no really satisfactory move.

19. Q—R5!
In the matter of an eye for combinative possibilities Tarrasch was no better than Steinitz. The move he makes is good and sound, but he overlooks that the fruit of his fine manœuvring, especially his provocation of Black's P—QB3, could have been plucked here and now by 19. P × P!, e.g.

A. 19. .... P × P. This is the only logical move but it is refuted combinatively as follows: 20. B × Kt ch, K × B; 21. Kt—Kt5!, P × Kt; 22. Q—Q5 ch, B—K3; 23. Q × R (23. .... B—K2; 24. Q × P). White is the Exchange ahead.

B. 19. .... B × P; 20. Kt—Kt5
  (1) 20. .... Q—Q1; 21. B × Kt ch, K × B; 22. QKt × QP ch and White wins with ease.
  (2) 20. .... B × Kt; 21. B × B ch, again with an easily won game for White.

C. 19. .... Q × P. Now there is no immediate decision but it is self-evident that the weak black Q-pawn, combined with White's control of Q5 and his great lead in development, will add up to a white win.

19. .... P—B4
The immediate danger is averted but Black is still badly placed.

20. B—QKt5!
Thus White gets rid of his bad Bishop in exchange for White's good one.

20. .... B × B
21. Kt × B Q—Kt3
22. Q—K2 Kt—B5
If 22. .... P—QR3; 23. Kt—B3, Q × P the simplest line would be 24. Kt—QR4!, Q—Kt4; 25. Q × Q ch, P × Q; 26. Kt—B3,

R—R4; 27. KR—QKt1, and White regains his pawn with decisive positional advantage.

23. Q—B4

After 23. B × Kt, P × B Black would have K4 available for his remaining Knight.

23.	P—QR3
24. Kt—B3	Q—Q1

Directed against 25. P—QKt4. If 24. .... Q × P the answer would again be 25. Kt—QR4!, etc.

25. P—KKt3	P—KKt3
26. Kt—KR4	

White could have won a pawn here without danger by 26. P × Kt, P × Kt; 27. KP × P. But Tarrasch generally refrained from any sort of liquidation so long as he could see chances of tying his opponent up still further.

26.	Kt—R4
27. P—QKt4	

This rapidly brings about a decisive opening of files on the Q-side.

27.	P—QKt4
28. Q—K2	B—K2

Third time lucky! 28. .... P—B5 would be met by 29. P—R4.

29. Kt—Kt2	Kt—Kt2
30. QR—Kt1	0—0
31. P—QR4	BP × P
32. R × P	Q—B2
33. B—Q2	P × P
34. R(1)—QKt1	

Winning at least a pawn.

34.	B—Q1

Black could have held out

longer by 34. .... KR—Kt1; but even this would have cost a pawn because after 35. R × R ch, R × R; 36. R × R ch, Q × R the White Queen captures both QR-pawns.

35. R × P	P—QR4
36. Q—Kt5	P—B4
37. R—B4	Q—K2
38. B—K3!	

Threatening to win a piece by 39. Q—B6.

38.	Q—K1
39. Q—Kt7	B—B3
40. B—R7	

In order to maintain his Queen at Kt7 White rules out R—Kt1 by Black.

40.	Kt—Kt4
41. Kt—Kt5	Kt—B2

A blunder in a hopeless position.

42. Kt—B7	R × B
43. Q × R?	

Under time pressure White overlooks that by 43. Kt × Q! he could win not merely the Exchange but a whole Rook: 43. .... R × Q; 44. Kt × B ch, K—R1; 45. R × R. This is the kind of slip one can easily make when in time trouble.

43.	Q—Q2
44. Q × P	

There was a quicker win by 44. R—Kt7 (44. .... Kt—Q1; 45. R—Kt8).

44.	Kt—Kt4

Black has obtained a not altogether harmless counter-attack.

45. Q—R4	Q—B2
46. R—Kt7	P × P
47. Q—R7	B—K2

For the fourth time Black plays B—K2; this time there is a little pitfall involved.

48. R—B3!

But White is not to be caught. After 48. Kt—K6?, Kt(2) × Kt Black would win; e.g.

A. 49. P × Kt, Kt—B6 ch; 50. K—R1, Q × P; 51. P—Kt4, Q × R, etc.

B. 49. R × B, Kt—B6 ch; 50. K—

R1, Q—B4; 51. P—Kt4, Q—Kt4;
(1) 52. Kt—K3, Q—Q5, etc.
(2) 52. Q—K3, Q × R; 53. P × Kt, P—Q4, etc.

48.	Kt—B6 ch
49. R × Kt!	P × R
50. Kt—K3	Q—B3
51. Kt—K6	Kt × Kt
52. R × B	

Now after any move of the Knight White will win by 53. Kt—Kt4.

Black resigns.

GAME 23

Emanuel Lasker (1868–1941), who succeeded Steinitz as World Champion, was a very different kind of virtuoso from Tarrasch. His technique contrasted in every respect. He never concerned himself much about any particularly deep planning. In the opening all that he asked was a reasonably decent position; a shade the better, a shade the worse, this mattered little to him. Only with the arrival of the middle-game complications and dangers did his genius awaken. Then he really could discover the best moves, or at least the most promising ones— especially when he was courting danger—and this was his real greatness. Uncommonly strong nerves seem to have been the basis of his powers. Above all he was practical—more so than Tarrasch and far more so than Steinitz.

His theoretical writings are very vague; they smack more of philosophy than chess technique. It is not possible to learn much from him; one can only stand and wonder.

As for his practical proficiency, it must be said that few World Champions could point to so imposing a record as his. He held the supreme title for no less a period than twenty-seven years!

The following game is a magnificent example of his skill in the handling of complications.

White: EMANUEL LASKER   Black: W. E. NAPIER

Cambridge Springs, 1904. *Sicilian Defence*

1. P—K4	P—QB4	5. Kt × P	B—Kt2
2. Kt—QB3	Kt—QB3	6. B—K3	P—Q3
3. Kt—B3	P—KKt3	7. P—KR3	Kt—B3
4. P—Q4	P × P	8. P—KKt4	

Lasker liked to play the Dragon Variation himself and he knew from Black's point of view the importance of achieving P—Q4. Hence this move of his, the chief object of which is to drive away the K-Knight from its place by 9. P—KKt5 and thus make P—Q4 difficult for Black. It is an interesting idea, if not an altogether safe one.

8. ....   0—0

Correct. Black is now threatening 9. .... P—Q4 with a good game. Had he played 8. .... P—Q4 directly, White would have got the advantage by 9. B—QKt5.

9. P—Kt5   Kt—K1
10. P—KR4

White combines his objectives in the centre with threats against the K-side, the idea being that if in spite of everything Black should succeed in forcing P—Q4 White will have another useful trump in hand.

10. ....   Kt—B2
11. P—B4

So as to be able to answer 11. .... P—Q4 with 12. P—K5.

11. ....   P—K4!

Excellent. Black changes his tack and gets good counter-play in the centre after all.

12. Kt(4)—K2

It is clear that either 12. Kt × Kt or 12. P × P would be playing Black's game.

12. ....   P—Q4?

A smart move, full of chances, but not correct. By the quiet

12. .... B—Kt5 Black could have guaranteed himself a good game. The extraordinary complications which now follow bring out the best in Lasker.

13. KP × P
13. Kt × P?, P × P! would favour Black.

13. ....   Kt—Q5!
14. Kt × Kt!

The best moves on both sides. After 14. B × Kt?, P × B; 15. Kt × P, Kt × P Black would have full compensation for the sacrificed pawn.

14. ....   Kt × P!

Another very fine move. After 14. .... P × Kt?, 15. B × P White would maintain his two extra pawns without much danger.

15. Kt—B5!

Apparently winning a piece.

15. ....   Kt × Kt!

The final point of 12. .... P—Q4; Black maintains material equality with a promising position.

16. Q × Q   R × Q
17. Kt—K7 ch!

Either 17. P × Kt?, B × Kt; or 17. Kt × B, Kt—Q4! would have left Black with the better of it.

17. ....   K—R1!

Both sides are consistently finding the best moves. After 17. .... K—B1?; 18. B—B5!, Kt—K5; 19. B—QR3, White would have had a powerful game. But now it does look as though after all Black is going to come out on top.

18. P—R5!!

46

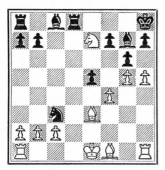

At this most critical juncture White plays a completely unexpected trump card and again upsets the chances. 18. Kt × B?, Kt—Q4! would be bad for White; and so would 18. P × Kt?, P × P; 19. B—Q4, B × B; 20. P × B, R—K1, etc.

18. ....   R—K1
19. B—B5   KtP × P!

In this way Black retains good chances even now. 19. .... KP × P on the other hand, though no less complicated, would have been more favourable to White; e.g.

A. 20. P × Kt?

(1) 20. .... B × P ch?; 21. K—B2, B × R; 22. B—B4, and White has an irresistible attack. The prettiest variation would be 22. .... B—B6; 23. B × BP, R × Kt; 24. P × P!, R × B; 25. P × R, B—Kt2; 26. P—Kt6, P—KR3; 27. R × P ch, B × R; 28. B—Q4 ch, B—Kt2; 29. P—B8(Q) mate.

(2) 20. .... R × Kt ch!; 21. B × R, B × P ch; 22. K—B2, B × R; 23. B—B4, B—

Q5 ch; 24. K—B3, B—KB4; and Black has the better chances.

B. 20. P × P!, P × P; 21. B—B4!, P—Kt4!; 22. B—B7, B—Kt2; 23. R—R2, Kt—Q4; 24. B × R, R × B; 25. 0—0—0 with decisive advantage to White.

20. B—B4!
After 20. P × Kt, B—B1; 21. B—Kt5, R × Kt etc., Black would have full compensation for the loss of the Exchange.

20. ....   P × P!
Again played in fine combinative style. Black handles the game no less brilliantly than his opponent. If he is to be worsted in the end, this result was already in the position after his twelfth move.

If 20. .... B—K3? White gets a decisive advantage as follows: 21. B × B, P × B; 22. P × Kt, B—B1!; 23. B—Q6! and now:

A. 23. .... B × Kt; 24. B × P ch, K—Kt1; 25. R × P, etc.

B. 23. .... P × P; 24. B—K5 ch, B—Kt2; 25. B—B6!, etc.

21. B × BP
At this point Lasker had only three minutes for his next ten moves. In view of the difficulty of the position he is thus in crushing time trouble.

21. ....   Kt—K5
22. B × R   B × P
23. R—QKt1   B—B6 ch
24. K—B1   B—KKt5!
Black is a whole Rook down. The outcome of his last combination however is that he is directly attacking both white Bishops and

indirectly attacking both white Rooks. Since he also has two extra pawns the situation still looks bright for him.

25. B × KRP!!
Lasker's clear insight into the combination and his fine flair for a favourable liquidation have found the right method for him. He gives back his Rook in such a way that he definitely takes control and rapidly emerges a pawn ahead.

25. ....   B × B
There is nothing better. After 25. .... Kt—Kt6 ch; 26. K—B2 there would follow either

A. 26. .... B × B; 27. R × B! running into the actual game; or else

B. 26. .... Kt × B?; 27. R × Kt! with even greater advantage to White.

26. R × B   Kt—Kt6 ch
27. K—Kt2   Kt × R
28. R × P
The scene is completely changed. The complications are over and the material is level, but all the white pieces are better placed than the Black ones. Black's QR-pawn is attacked and his KB-pawn is very weak.

28. ....   P—R4
29. R—Kt3!   B—Kt2
30. R—KR3!
With this last move under time-pressure White reopens his attack down the KR-file. The battle is over.

30. ....   Kt—Kt6
31. K—B3
This wins the B-pawn, for either 31. .... B—K4? or 31. .... R—KB1? would fail against 32. Kt—Kt6 ch.

31. ....   R—R3
32. K × P   Kt—K7 ch
33. K—B5   Kt—B6
34. P—R3   Kt—R5
35. B—K3
With the unanswerable threat of 36. P—Kt6, e.g. 35. .... B—B1; 36. B—Q4 ch, B—Kt2; 37. P—Kt6!, etc. Black resigns.

GAME 24

One of the best of the virtuosi was the American Harry Pillsbury (1872–1906). He specialized in K-side attacks on a positional basis, and his deadliest weapon was the breakthrough—the combinative opening of lines into the enemy stronghold. Game 19 has already given some idea of Pillsbury's talent, even though in that game he figured as the loser. Here is his 'Immortal Game'.

White: H. N. PILLSBURY   Black: EM. LASKER
Nuremberg, 1896. *French Defence*

1. P—K4	P—K3
2. P—Q4	P—Q4
3. Kt—QB3	Kt—KB3
4. P—K5	KKt—Q2
5. P—B4	P—QB4

| 6. P × P | Kt—QB3 |
| 7. P—QR3 | Kt × BP |

More incisive than 7. .... B × P.

8. P—QKt4   Kt—Q2?

Inconsequent. The correct line of play, according to Lasker, was 8. .... P—Q5; 9. QKt—K2, P—Q6!; 10. Kt—Kt3, Q—Q5 with promising play.

9. B—Q3   P—QR4

Risky play. Black gets control of his QB4 but loses several tempi.

10. P—Kt5   Kt(3)—Kt1
11. Kt—B3   Kt—B4
12. B—K3   Kt(1)—Q2
13. 0—0   P—KKt3

Preventing 14. P—B5.

14. Kt—K2   B—K2

Black decides that his King will be safest in the centre. The text move, however, hampers the co-operation of the black pieces. It seems that after all 14. .... B—Kt2 followed by 0—0 would have been better.

15. Q—K1   Kt—Kt3
16. Kt(3)—Q4   B—Q2
17. Q—B2

Threatening 18. Kt × P, winning a pawn.

17. ....   Kt(3)—R5

Here Black would have done better to set about occupying QB5 by 17. .... Q—B2 followed by Kt(4)—R5 and Kt(3)—B5.

18. QR—Kt1

Otherwise it would not have been easy to prevent the loss of a pawn after 18. .... Kt—Kt7; but White's move also has an attacking point, as will presently appear.

18. ....   P—R4

Black is still convinced that his King is safest in the middle; but even now castling would have given better chances. On the other hand the attempt to win a pawn by 18. .... Kt × B; 19. P × Kt, B × RP? would have cost a piece: 20. R—R1, Q—K2; 21. Kt—B2, etc.

19. P—Kt6!

In order to restrict still more the already limited mobility of the black pieces. The advantages involved in the text move carry far more weight than the QR-pawn which White is sacrificing.

19. ....   Kt × B

After 19. .... Kt × P White regains the pawn advantageously by 20. Kt × P!

20. P × Kt   B × P

Now this is no blunder, for the Knight is protected, so that 21. R—R1 would achieve nothing.

21. P—B5!

A little breakthrough in preparation for the big one to come. The square KB4 is being vacated for the Knight on K2.

Pillsbury possessed an unparalleled technique when it came to unleashing the explosive powers of his pieces.

21. ....   KtP × P

After 21. .... KP × P; 22. Kt—B4 White wins easily.

22. Kt—B4

Now there are several combinative possibilities in the air; e.g. Q—Kt3—Kt7; or 23. Q—B3,

P—R5; 24. Kt × BP, P × Kt;
25. Kt × P, etc.

22. ....   P—R5
To prevent 23. Q—Kt3 and at
the same time forestall 23. Q—
B3.

23. R—R1!
The prelude to a combination
of rare depth which produces a
more clear-cut result than the
line 23. Kt × BP, P × Kt;
24. Kt × P—promising though
that also is.

23. ....   B—K2
23. .... B—B1 comes to
much the same thing, while
23. .... Q—K2 is refuted
simply by 24. Kt × BP, etc.

24. R × Kt!!
To take a guard from the K-
pawn.

24. ....   B × R
25. Kt(Q4) × KP!! P × Kt
26. Kt × KP

47

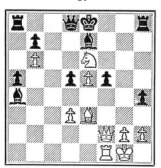

The great virtuoso of the
breakthrough presents his *chef
d'œuvre*. Black, a clear Rook
ahead, must now lose, play as he
will. To have foreseen all this is

a brilliant piece of work by
Pillsbury. There are few combinations on record to be compared with it.

26. ....   B—Q2
Black sees that he can only
prolong the game—not save it.
After 26. .... Q—B1; 27. Q ×
BP!, with the main threat of
28. B—Kt5! White would win
more quickly; e.g.

A. 27. .... R—KKt1; 28. Q—
B7 ch, K—Q2; 29. Kt—B5 ch,
etc.

B. 27. .... Q—B3; 28. B—
Kt5!, Q × P ch; 29. P—Q4, Q—
Kt5; 30. Q—B7 ch, K—Q2;
31. B × B, Q × B; 32. Kt—B5 ch,
K—Q1; 33. Kt × P ch, K—Q2;
P—K6 ch, etc.

27. Kt × Q   R × Kt
Black has only Rook and
Bishop for the Queen. Moreover
his pawns are horribly weakened
and his King is still insecure.
The rest is simple.

28. B—B5   R—QB1
29. B × B   K × B
30. Q—K3   R—B3
31. Q—Kt5 ch   K—B2
32. R—B1   R × R ch
33. Q × R   R—QB1
34. Q—K1   P—R6
The immediate advance of the
other Rook-pawn is also useless;
e.g. 34. .... P—R5; 35. Q × P,
P—R6; 36. Q—R7 ch, and now:

A. 36. .... K—K3; 37. Q—
Kt7! and wins.

B. 36. .... K—K1; 37. Q—
Kt6 ch
  (1) 37. .... K—B1; 38. Q—
      Q6 ch, K—K1; 39. Q ×
      RP and wins.

(2) 37. .... K—K2; 38. Q—
B6 ch, K—K1; 39. P—
K6 and wins.

(3) 37. .... K—Q1; 38. Q—
B6 ch, K—K1; 39. P—
K6 and wins.

35. P × P	R—Kt1 ch	39. Q × P	R × P
36. K—B2	P—R5	40. Q—B5	R—K3
37. Q—Kt4	R—Kt3	41. Q—B7	K—K2
38. K—B3	P—R6	42. K—B4	P—Kt3
		43. P—R4	R—QB3
		44. Q—Kt8	B—K1
		45. K × P	R—R3
		46. Q—B7 ch	K—B1
		47. Q—Q8	P—Kt4
		48. P—K6	R—R2
		49. K—K5	P—Kt5
		50. Q—Q6 ch	Resigns.

GAME 25

Frank Marshall (1877–1944) was one of the leaders of a group of tacticians who remained faithful to the chess of the 19th century—the golden age of combination. Not that Marshall rejected the principles of modern position play; he applied them as it were en passant *but laid no emphasis on them, and he kicked over the traces with alacrity whenever he saw a chance. The result was a large number of pretty sacrificial games which in the context of advancing chess theory may seem anachronistic but which nevertheless bear witness to the rich potentialities of the game.*

White: S. M. LEWITZKY   Black: F. J. MARSHALL
Breslau, 1912.   *French Defence*

1. P—Q4	P—K3
2. P—K4	P—Q4
3. Kt—QB3	P—QB4

A challenging move, typical of Marshall's style.

4. Kt—B3
White declines to take up the challenge. The obvious line is 4. KP × P, KP × P; 5. P × P, after which 5. .... P—Q5 is not good, according to present-day theory, because of 6. B—Kt5 ch, Kt—B3; 7. B × Kt ch, P × B; 8. QKt—K2. Marshall would probably have played 5. .... B—K3 (as he does later in the present game) hoping that his swift development would compensate for the lost pawn.

4.	Kt—QB3
5. KP × P	KP × P
6. B—K2	

The move 6. P × P was still to be considered.

6.	Kt—B3
7. O—O	B—K2
8. B—KKt5	O—O
9. P × P	B—K3

After 9. .... P—Q5 White would have a very strong continuation in 10. B × Kt, B × B; 11. Kt—K4.

10. Kt—Q4
Nor can White hold the gambit pawn by 10. Kt—QR4, because of the answer 10. .... Kt—K5.

10. ....   B × P
11. Kt × B

This exchange would be advantageous only if White could immediately attack the black Q-pawn by P—QB4. As this is not the case, it is Black who benefits by the opening of the KB-file. White should have chosen 11. B—K3.

11. ....   P × Kt
12. B—Kt4   Q—Q3
13. B—R3   QR—K1
14. Q—Q2

White is already in some difficulty. 14. R—K1 is bad because of the reply B × P ch! But 14. Q—Q3 would have been better than the move played.

14. ....   B—Kt5!

A very nasty pin for White, who is now threatened both with 15. .... P—Q5 and 15. .... Kt—K5.

15. B × Kt
Practically forced.

15. ....   R × B
16. QR—Q1   Q—B4
17. Q—K2

White gives up a pawn on QB3, intending to regain it on Q5; but in the complications which result Marshall is far too good for his opponent.

17. ....   B × Kt
18. P × B   Q > P
19. R × P

So far it has been White's combination. Now it is Black's turn.

19. ....   Kt—Q5!
20. Q—R5?

Missing the mark! 20. Q—K5 would have been even worse because of 20. .... Kt—B6 ch!; 21. P × Kt, R—Kt3 ch; 22. B—Kt2, Q × KBP, etc. White must therefore try 20. Q—K4. Then follows 20. .... R—B5!; 21. Q—K5, Q—Q7 (preventing 22. R—Q7 because of the reply 22. .... Kt—K7 ch); 22. R—QB5, Kt—K7 ch; 23. K—R1, R × P! Now it does look as though Black will get the better of it after all, but White can at least still fight on by 24. Q—R1, which averts all the immediate dangers.

20. ....   R(1)—KB1

With the double threat of 21. .... P × R and 21. .... R × P (22. R × R, Q—K8 ch).

21. R—K5

White parries both threats but now comes a blow from the other side.

21. ....   R—R3!
22. Q—Kt5

White sees that 22. Q—Q1 would be refuted by 22. .... Kt—B6 ch followed by 23. .... Q × R.

22. ....   R × B!

Thus Black wins a piece. White cannot recapture because of 23. .... Kt—B6 ch.

23. R—QB5

Apparently giving Black a little trouble even yet. But Marshall solves the problem at a single stroke, with a most brilliant move.

23. ....   Q—KKt6!!
White resigns.

If 24. RP × Q there follows 24. .... Kt—K7 mate, while 24. BP × Q is followed by 24. .... Kt—K7 ch and mate next move. Finally 24. Q × Q leads to 24. .... Kt—K7 ch; 25. K—R1, Kt × Q ch; not mate this time, but after 26. K—Kt1, Kt × R (or 26. .... Kt—K7 ch) White's game is utterly lost.

48

GAME 26

As the standard of technique continued to rise, smaller and smaller niceties had to be taken into account. Even the most insignificant little peculiarities of a position were taken up with the hope of nursing them into 'grown-up' features of the game. The first outstanding master to achieve practical successes on this basis, by his eye for the microscopic advantage, his endless patience and his indomitable fighting spirit was Geza Maróczy (1870–1951). He can be considered as the forerunner of various other strategists—especially Rubinstein.

Since microscopic considerations can hardly play much part in lively positions Maróczy mostly made capital out of his technique in the handling of simple positions. His speciality was the Queen and pawns ending, in which he was the greatest expert of all.

Here is one of his best and most characteristic games.

White: G. MARÓCZY   Black: F. J. MARSHALL

Carlsbad, 1907.   *Four Knights*

1. P—K4	P—K4
2. Kt—KB3	Kt—QB3
3. Kt—B3	Kt—B3
4. B—Kt5	Kt—Q5
5. Kt × P	B—Kt5

5. .... Q—K2 is best here.

6. B—K2	Q—K2

Necessary; otherwise Black will not regain his pawn.

7. Kt—Q3	B × Kt
8. QP × B	Kt × B
9. Q × Kt	Q × P

It looks as though the game is already as good as drawn.

10. B—K3!
With this move White keeps the game alive.

10. ....   0—0
If 10. .... Q × P? there follows 11. B—Q4 ch, Q—K5; 12. R—KKt1! with advantage to White: e.g. 12. .... Q × Q ch; 13. K × Q, K—B1; 14. R × P!, K × R; 15. R—Kt1 ch,

K—B1; 16. B × Kt, R—KKt1;
17. B—K7 ch, etc.

11. O—O—O   P—Q3
Taking the Kt-pawn would
now involve even worse problems
than at the previous move.

12. P—B3   Q—QB5
13. B—Q4!
Yet another pawn offer which
Black cannot accept.

13. ....   R—K1
After 13. .... Q × RP? White
would get the upper hand by
14. B × Kt, P × B; 15. Q—K7.

14. Q—B2   B—B4
Still not 14. .... Q × RP?
because of 15. KR—K1, after
which Black has no satisfactory
way of meeting the twin threats
of 16. Q—Kt3 and 16. B × Kt.

15. P—QKt3   Q—R3
16. B × Kt   B × Kt
17. R × B   P × B
18. K—Kt2
White has achieved only the
slightest edge. True he has
broken up the black K-side but
it is not clear how he can make
anything out of this. The means
for a K-side attack are completely lacking.

18. ....   R—K3
Black now threatens to make
himself master of the K-file.
This cannot be permitted.

19. R—K1   QR—K1
20. R(3)—K3   K—B1
Again one gets the impression
that the players might as well
quietly agree to a draw. But to
Maróczy a chance is still discernible.

21. R × R   R × R
22. R × R
He even goes so far as to rid
Black of his doubled pawn.

22. ....   P × R
23. Q—R4!

49

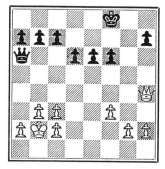

Only now does a faint idea of
White's intentions begin to dawn.
The white Queen on KR4 is more
active than the black Queen on
QR3, while the white King on
QKt2 is safer than the black
King on KB1.

But to make capital out of this
would require the patience of a
saint and—even more important
—the technique of a Maróczy!

23. ....   K—Kt2
24. Q—Kt4 ch   K—B2
25. Q—R5 ch   K—Kt2
26. Q—K8
It begins to look as though he
is achieving something.

26. ....   Q—K7!
But now it seems that it will
come to nothing after all, for the
black Queen also bursts into
violent action.

27. Q—K7 ch   K—Kt3
28. Q—B8!

Indirectly protecting the KKt-pawn. The real difference between the activity of the two Queens is this: White can choose between attack and defence, and thus direct the course of affairs.

After 28. Q × BP, Q × KtP Black would rapidly have achieved something of great importance in such endgames—something which is enough to counterbalance several pawn losses—a fleet-footed passed pawn.

28.	P—K4
29. Q—Kt8 ch	K—R3
30. Q—B8 ch	K—Kt3
31. Q—Kt8 ch	K—R3
32. P—KR4!	

After some repetition of moves to gain time White proceeds to strengthen his position with a very fine manœuvre.

32.	Q—B7
33. Q—B8 ch	K—Kt3
34. P—R5 ch!	K × P
35. Q—Kt7!	

This was the intention behind 32. P—R4! The black KR-pawn must now fall, and the indirect exchange of the two KR-pawns gives White a new small advantage, as immediately appears.

| 35. .... | Q—Q7 |

35. .... P—KB4; 36. Q × P ch, K—Kt4; 37. Q—Kt7 ch also favours White. Maróczy gives the following variations:

A. 37. .... K—R4; 38. P—Kt4 ch, P × P; 39. P × P ch, K—R5; 40. P—Kt5, P—K5; 41. P—Kt6, P—K6; 42. Q—R7 ch, K—Kt6; 43. P—Kt7 and wins.

B. 37. .... K—B5; 38. Q—

R6 ch, K—Kt6; 39. Q—Kt5 ch, K—R7; 40. P—KKt4, P × P; 41. P × P, P—K5; 42. Q—R6 ch!, K—Kt7; 43. P—Kt5,

(1) 43. .... Q—B5; 44. Q—B6, Q × Q; 45. P × Q, P—K6; 46. P—B7, P—K7; 47. P—B8(Q), P—K8(Q); 48. Q—Kt7 ch, and White wins two pawns.

(2) 43. .... P—K6; 44. P—Kt6, P—K7; 45. Q—Kt5 ch!, K—B8!; 46. P—Kt7, P—K8(Q); 47. P—Kt8(Q), and Black cannot avoid the loss of a pawn; e.g. 47. .... Q(K8)—K7; 48. Q—B1 ch, Q(K7)—K8; 49. Q—QB4 ch, etc.

36. Q × P ch	Q—R3
37. P—Kt4 ch	K—Kt4
38. Q × P	

Now White has established material superiority under favourable circumstances, the KR-pawns having vanished. But the win is still difficult enough.

38.	K—B5
39. Q × KtP	Q—R8
40. Q—Kt4 ch	K × P
41. Q × P	K × P
42. P—B4!	

White's winning method is based on the rapid advance of this pawn. After 42. Q × P, Q—Q4! (43. P—B4, Q—Q5 ch!); the win would be much more difficult, if not, indeed, impossible.

| 42. .... | P—K5 |
| 43. P—B5 | P—B4 |

Black is compelled to lose an important tempo in the promotion race; after 43. .... P—K6? the pawn would be lost by 44. Q—Q4 ch! for 44. .... K—

B6? loses the Queen by 45. Q—Q5 ch.

44. P—B6   Q—R1 ch

Maróczy demonstrated that this interpolation is also necessary, for 44. .... P—K6 leads to a forced loss as follows: 45. Q—Q4 ch, Q—K5; 46. Q × Q ch!, P × Q; 47. P—B7, P—K7; 48. P—B8(Q) ch, K—B6; 49. Q—B8 ch, K—Kt7; 50. Q—Kt4, K—B7; 51. Q × P(4), etc.

45. P—B3   P—K6
46. Q—Kt6 ch!

By driving the black King to B5 he prevents the possibility of Black winning the pawn as soon as it reaches B7 by checking at KR7; e.g. 46. P—B7, P—K7; 47. Q—K6? (47. Q—Kt6 ch!); 47. .... P—K8(Q); 48. Q × Q, Q—R2 ch followed by 49. .... Q × BP with a probable draw.

46. ....   K—B5
47. P—B7   P—K7
48. Q—K6   K—B6

The only move, for 48. .... P—K8(Q) is now useless, and 48. .... Q—R7? fails against 49. Q—Q6 ch!

49. Q × BP ch   K—Kt7

50. Q—Kt4 ch   K—B7
51. Q—B4 ch   K—Kt7
52. Q—K3!   K—B8
53. Q—B3 ch   K—K8

Now that Black has been forced to block his own passed pawn the win is there for the taking.

54. Q—B4

The problem can now be solved in several ways. The simplest, as Maróczy pointed out, would have been 54. Q—B5, K—Q7; 55. Q—Q7 ch, K—K6; 56. P—B8(Q), Q × Q; 57. Q × Q, P—K8(Q); 58. Q—K8 ch, K—B7; 59. Q × Q ch, etc.

54. ....   Q—QB1
55. Q—Q6   K—B7
56. Q—Q8   P—K8(Q)

In order to give a few little checks. If 56. .... Q × Q; 57. P × Q(Q), P—K8(Q); White has the decisive continuation 58. Q—R4 ch; and of course 56. .... Q × P is just as hopeless (57. Q × Q, P—K8(Q); 58. Q × P ch, etc.).

57. Q × Q   Q—Q7 ch
58. K—R3   Q—B8 ch
59. K—R4   Q—B5 ch
60. P—B4   Resigns.

GAME 27

Akiba Rubinstein (1882–1961) was one of the strongest representatives of the Steinitz school. He also knew how to apply—with understanding and refinement—all the practical rules devised by Tarrasch. In every respect he was a player of exceptional ability. Not only had he combinative talent beyond the ordinary but he also possessed an almost supernatural feeling for the endgame, and for Rook endings in particular.

Rubinstein probably has to his name more model games than any other player—flawless endgames and also fantastic attacks studded with all manner of sacrifices.

In the years preceding the First World War Rubinstein was considered a most worthy crown prince of the chess world, and it is an unfortunate fact that only financial difficulties deprived him of a much-desired match for the world title.

White: G. A. ROTLEWI   Black: A. RUBINSTEIN

Lodz, 1908.   *Queen's Gambit Declined*

1. P—Q4	P—Q4
2. Kt—KB3	P—K3
3. P—K3	P—QB4
4. P—B4	Kt—QB3
5. Kt—B3	Kt—B3
6. QP × P	

This giving up of the centre followed by fianchetto of the Q-Bishop used to be very popular; nowadays it is not considered very effective.

6.	B × P
7. P—QR3	P—QR3
8. P—QKt4	B—Q3
9. B—Kt2	0—0
10. Q—Q2	

This is no good place for the Queen. As White will very soon have to move this piece elsewhere the text amounts to loss of time. Better 10. P × P followed by 11. B—K2.

10.	Q—K2
11. B—Q3	

After 11. P × P, P × P; 12. Kt × P, Kt × Kt; 13. Q × Kt, B—K3! Black will have ample compensa-

tion for the pawn (14. Q—Q1, Kt × P!; or 14. Q—KKt5, B × P ch!).

11.	P × P
12. B × P	P—QKt4
13. B—Q3	R—Q1
14. Q—K2	B—Kt2
15. 0—0	Kt—K4!

Black has gained two tempi and now opens his attack.

16. Kt × Kt	B × Kt
17. P—B4	

White makes a virtue of necessity and hopes that through this central advance he may yet be able to get his own attack in first. His appraisal of the situation however turns out to be far too optimistic.

17.	B—B2
18. P—K4?	

The logical continuation, but ruinous.

18. .... QR—B1	

Quite correctly Black makes

no attempt to deter White from his ill-conceived plan.

19. P—K5?

White's final presumptuous move, and it leads to a forced loss. Rubinstein now acquits himself of his task in inimitably beautiful style. The principle is simple enough: Black throws every single piece into the battle, and White, with his development still incomplete, is unable to beat off the onslaught.

19. ....   B—Kt3 ch
20. K—R1   Kt—Kt5!

50

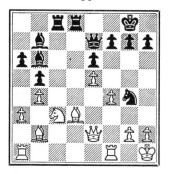

This first offer is no more than a pseudo-sacrifice. After 21. Q × Kt, R × B; Black would threaten not only 22. .... R(6) × Kt but also 22. .... R—Q7. Nor would the interpolated check at KR7 help: 21. B × P ch, K × B; 22. Q × Kt, R—Q7, etc. In both cases White would have an untenable position.

21. B—K4

Hoping to stem the flood by exchanges. 21. Kt—K4 would be quite useless: 21. .... R × B; 22. Q × R, B × Kt; 23. Q × B, Q—R5; 24. P—R3, Q—Kt6!, etc.

21. ....   Q—R5
22. P—Kt3

The other main line is 22. P—R3. Then follows 22. .... R × Kt! with the following possibilities:

A. 23. B × B?, R × RP ch and mate follows.

B. 23. Q × Kt, R × RP ch; 24. Q × R, Q × Q ch; 25. P × Q, B × B ch; 26. K—R2, R—Q7 ch; 27. K—Kt3, R—Kt7 ch; 28. K—R4, B—Q1 ch; 29. K—R5, B—Kt3 mate.

C. 23. B × R, B × B; 24. Q × Kt (24. Q × B, Q—Kt6, etc.) 24. .... Q × Q; 25. P × Q, R—Q6; 26. K—R2, R × B; and Black is ahead on material. After the text move the storm really breaks.

22. ....   R × Kt!!
Queen sacrifice!

51

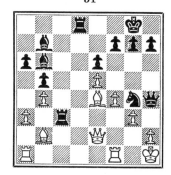

23. P × Q
Other possibilities:

A. 23. B × R, B × B ch; 24. Q × B, Q × P mate.

B. 23. B × B, R × P;
  (1) 24.   B—KB3,   Kt × RP;
      25. Q × Kt, R—R6, etc.

(2) 24.   QR—Q1,   R × R;
25. R × R, R—R6, etc.
(3) 24. R—B3, R × R; 25. B ×
R, Kt—B7 ch; 26. K—Kt1,
(26.   K—Kt2,   Q—R6 ch)
26.   ....   Kt—K5 ch;
27.   K—B1,   Kt—Q7 ch;
28.   K—Kt2,   Kt × B;
29. Q × Kt, R—Q7 ch.

23. ....   R—Q7!!

24. Q × R
What else? After 24. B × B
Black continues decisively with
24.   ....   R × Q; 25. B—Kt2,
R—R6!

24. ....   B × B ch
25. Q—Kt2   R—R6
A wonderful finishing touch.
Mate is inevitable, and White
resigns. This is Rubinstein's
immortal game.

GAME 28

*José Raoul Capablanca (1888–1942) was one of the most talented
players in the whole history of chess. In the endgame and in pure
position play Capablanca had no peer, and because of this the idea
has arisen that as a tactician he was no better than his contemporaries.
This is quite untrue. In his best years (from 25 to 40) Capablanca was
feared most of all for the speed and depth of his penetration into every
kind of position, even the most complex.*

*His only weak point was the openings. He had neither the patience
nor the diligence to apply himself, day in, day out, to the study of
openings, the five-finger exercises of the chess player. This is why
Alekhine, in his match with Capablanca in 1927, put the accent on
the openings. When he succeeded in extracting some tiny advantage
he settled down to the long task of exploiting it by positional means.
As a tactician Capablanca was unsurpassable; his many meetings with
combinative players provide the proof.*

White: J. R. CAPABLANCA   Black: F. J. MARSHALL
New York, 1918. *Ruy Lopez: Marshall Gambit*

1. P—K4   P—K4
2. Kt—KB3   Kt—QB3
3. B—Kt5   P—QR3
4. B—R4   Kt—B3
5. 0—0   B—K2
6. R—K1   P—QKt4
7. B—Kt3   0—0
Or 7. .... P—Q3; 8. P—B3,
0—0; with transposition of
moves. But in the present case
7. .... 0—0 is played with an
entirely different intention.
Black is preparing a pawn sacri-

fice which will secure for him an
enduring initiative.

8. P—B3   P—Q4
The Marshall Gambit. Today's
theory considers it correct.

9. P × P   Kt × P
10. Kt × P   Kt × Kt
11. R × Kt
It says much for Marshall's
intuition that in this position he
considered Black to have sufficient compensation for the pawn.

This compensation, which is of a temporary nature, consists in:

A. Obstruction of White's development.

B. Rapid availability of all Black's minor pieces.

C. Attacking possibilities against the white K-side.

11. . . . .   Kt—B3
Later (much later) investigations have shown that the strongest move here is 11. . . . . P—QB3. One recent example from the Tal–Spassky match (Tiflis, 1965): 12. B × Kt, P × B; 13. P—Q4, B—Q3; 14. R—K3, Q—R5; 15. P—KR3, Q—B5; 16. R—K5, Q—B3; 17. R—K1, Q—Kt3; 18. Q—B3, B—K3; and Black's threats of Q—B7 and P—Kt5 maintain the equilibrium.

12. R—K1   B—Q3
The Black position does indeed look full of promise, and one can only marvel at Capablanca going into such a variation, knowing well that his opponent would be thoroughly versed in the coming complications. This is where the full grandeur of the Cuban appears. Although Capablanca is remembered as the positional player par excellence he was nevertheless, as we said in the introduction to this game, more than a match for the great combinative players when it came to cutting his way through a thicket of variations. This was particularly true when his opponent had sacrificed material in the interests of attack.

To Capablanca it was a point of honour to take up Marshall's challenge, and this is why he did not play P—Q3 at his ninth move.

13. P—KR3   Kt—Kt5
This is the most trenchant line; acceptance of this sacrifice would be hazardous in the extreme: 14. P × Kt, Q—R5; 15. Q—B3 (15. P—Kt3, B × P!) and now:

A. 15. . . . . Q—R7 ch; 16. K—B1, B × P? (obvious but insufficient) 17. Q × B, Q—R8 ch; 18. K—K2, QR—K1 ch; 19. B—K6!! and White wins.

B. 15. . . . . B × P; 16. P—Kt3!, Q—R4; 17. Q—R1, and White has survived the worst.

C. 15. . . . . B—R7 ch (best); 16. K—B1, B × P; and the black attack is very strong. (17. R—K4 fails against 17. . . . . B—B5!!)

14. Q—B3   Q—R5
15. P—Q4   Kt × P
A promising piece-sacrifice. If now 16. Q × Kt there follows, not 16. . . . . B—Kt6? because of 17. Q × P ch with mate to follow, but 16. . . . . B—R7 ch!; 17. K—B1, B—Kt6; with a winning attack. (18. Q × P ch?, R × Q ch!).

16. R—K2

52

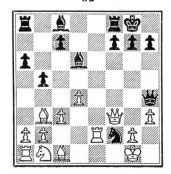

One stands amazed as the great Capablanca gives evidence of complete mastery of this complicated position. He often had to adopt safety-first tactics; whenever he was forced into escapades with his King—as in the present game—he could manage things to perfection in the midst of great dangers.

A good alternative here was 16. B—Q2.

| 16. .... | B—KKt5 |

Modern theory prefers 16. .... Kt—Kt5; with the possible sequel 17. R—K8, Kt—B3; 18. R × R ch, K × R; 19. Kt—Q2, R—Kt1; 20. Kt—B1, giving about even chances.

17. P × B

Or 17. Q × Kt, B—Kt6; 18. Q—B1, B × R; 19. Q × B, QR—K1; and wins.

| 17. .... | B—R7 ch |
| 18. K—B1 | B—Kt6 |

Marshall is continually confronting his opponent with new and embarrassing problems.

| 19. R × Kt | Q—R8 ch |
| 20. K—K2 | B × R |

After the obvious 20. .... Q × B there would follow 21. R—B1!, Q × P ch; 22. Kt—Q2, and White is perfectly safe. He could meet QR—K1 ch with K—Q3 and then, with a piece against a pawn, would have an easily won game.

| 21. B—Q2 | B—R5 |
| 22. Q—R3 | QR—K1 ch |

| 23. K—Q3 | Q—B8 ch |
| 24. K—B2 | B—B7 |

Black seeks in vain to find fresh points of contact for his attack.

25. Q—B3	Q—Kt8
26. B—Q5	P—QB4
27. P × P	B × P
28. P—Kt4	

The best preparation for the liberating move which follows.

| 28. .... | B—Q3 |
| 29. P—R4! | |

Thus White mobilizes his Rook as well, and thereby settles the argument.

| 29. .... | P—QR4 |
| 30. RP × P | RP × P |

Black strives to open the game to the utmost, in order to get at the white King.

31. R—R6	P × P
32. Kt × P	B—Kt5
33. P—Kt6	

Now White assumes the initiative.

33.	B × Kt
34. B × B	P—R3
35. P—Kt7	R—K6

Forlorn hope.

| 36. B × P ch | R × B |

If 36. .... K—R2 there follows 37. Q—B5 ch and mate in two.

37. P—Kt8(Q) ch

White mates in four: 37. .... K—R2; 38. R × P ch, K × R; 39. Q—R8 ch, K—Kt3; 40. Q—R5 mate.

During the last years before 1914 technique was becoming more and more a matter of routine. Within the prevailing conceptions of the time positional play was approaching its limit. A feeling that everything was now known and understood seemed to come over the leading masters, damping their fighting spirit and blurring and standardizing their playing style. They were tremendously strong players, these grandmasters (as they have come to be called) but many of their games were drawn by mutual consent, often without any apparent will to win. Capablanca himself was no exception.

As examples of this tendency here are two games (No. 29 and 30), without comment.

We do not wish to give the impression that these standard draws were characteristic of the youngest players of the period; we simply state the facts. It is indeed true that these 'last of the virtuosi' produced many immortal games—enough to fill a book; but the present book is not concerned with individual performances, only with the trend of the times.

GAME 29

White: C. SCHLECHTER   Black: R. TEICHMANN

San Sebastian, 1911. *French Defence*

1. P—K4	P—K3	11. B—Q2	P—B3
2. P—Q4	P—Q4	12. QKt—K2	B—Q3
3. Kt—QB3	Kt—KB3	13. B—B4	B × B
4. P × P	P × P	14. Kt × B	Q—Q3
5. B—KKt5	B—K2	15. Q—Q2	B—Q2
6. B—Q3	Kt—B3	16. KR—K1	KR—K1
7. KKt—K2	Kt—QKt5	17. P—KB3	R × R ch
8. 0—0	Kt × B	18. R × R	R—K1
9. Q × Kt	0—0	19. R × R ch	B × R
10. Kt—Kt3	P—KR3	Draw.	

GAME 30

White: J. R. CAPABLANCA   Black: O. DURAS

San Sebastian, 1911. *Queen's Gambit*

1. P—Q4	P—Q4	8. B—Kt2	Kt—B3
2. Kt—KB3	Kt—KB3	9. B—K2	P × P
3. P—K3	P—K3	10. B × P	P—QKt4
4. P—B4	B—K2	11. B—K2	Q × Q ch
5. Kt—B3	P—QR3	12. R × Q	B—Kt2
6. P—QKt3	P—B4	13. 0—0	K—K2
7. QP × P	B × P	14. Kt—Kt5	Kt—R2

15. R—B1	QR—QB1	23. Kt × P	R × R
16. KR—Q1	P—R3	24. B × R	Kt—K5
17. B—B3	B × B	25. Kt—Q2	Kt × Kt
18. Kt × B	KR—Q1	26. B × Kt	K—Q2
19. R × R	R × R	27. P—R3	K—B3
20. K—B1	B—Q3	28. K—Q3	Kt—Kt4
21. K—K2	R—QB1	29. P—B4	P—K4
22. P—QR4	P × P	Draw.	

THE INDEPENDENT THINKERS
Between the Wars: 1919–1940

This RECENT stage in the evolution of chess is sharply defined by the two Great Wars, one of which ended in November, 1918 and the other began in September, 1939. We shall refer to the leading players of this period as the inter-war masters, since they flourished between these two great upheavals. At the time when the new ideas were emerging their adherents were known as the moderns, or the hyper-moderns, or the neo-romantics, but as the period recedes into the past these names become less apposite.

It is a good and instructive thing to look back to the birth of modern chess thought. After the 1914–18 war, when inter-national chess was little by little becoming re-established, the style of several of the leading masters exhibited essential differences from that of the older generation. The chief protagonists of these new ideas were Alekhine, Bogolyubov, Breyer, Nimzovitch and Réti.

But was this really something quite new? Were these masters actually proclaiming a fresh gospel? We may put this question now, for the storm which the modern chess movement raised at the time has long died down and it is possible to look at the subject more calmly and objectively.

The two great pedagogues in the realm of chess throughout the fifty years beginning about 1870 were Steinitz and Tarrasch. Steinitz died in 1900 and Tarrasch may be considered his successor. In the foregoing chapter it has already been remarked that Tarrasch presented the teachings of Steinitz in more practical form. Strikingly didactic in his approach, he had the knack of reducing important principles to nice, easily-grasped rules, such as: 'develop the Knights first, then the Bishops'; 'the Bishop is stronger than the Knight'; 'don't play the same piece twice in the opening'; and so on. Such hints as these, coming from one who had for many years been scoring brilliant international successes, who could back up his rules with attractive examples, and whose ideas and opinions were quoted daily throughout the whole chess world, were bound, in course of time, to become chessplayers' maxims. This was going too far. Dogmatism began to supersede understanding. Inventiveness was being relegated to the background.

In these circumstances criticism of the prevailing style was inevitable. But the war broke out, and for five years international chess came to a standstill. There was no opportunity for reformation to be gradual; hence the extraordinary impact of the various strategic innovations of the young masters of 1918. The enthusiasm with which these revolutionary novelties were greeted led to a somewhat exaggerated idea of their significance, but the fact remains that these were lovely, enthralling times, and they found a worthy memorial in Réti's book *Modern Ideas in Chess*.

In all this, however, what was really new? From the historical point of view it would seem that all the old dogmas had suddenly collapsed in face of modern matter-of-fact objectivity. The Queen must not be moved early in the game? The centre pawns must be advanced as rapidly as possible? No piece should be moved twice in the opening? Ha! Ha! The neo-romantics demonstrated over and over again that all these rules can be broken with impunity and even with advantage, in appropriate circumstances.

It emerged that these circumstances were far more frequent than had previously been supposed. It was not that the old rules had been refuted; rather it had been realized that they had formerly been followed too slavishly. So away with drowsy wood-shifting! The modern masters met every situation with stark objectivity. Especially in the build-up stage they found many opportunities of successfully replacing old schemes with unconventional but more appropriate moves and manœuvres, and soon a whole range of new openings and variations sprang up.

The most important of these modern conceptions concerned the strategy of the centre. Two fundamental propositions emerge; namely that what matters is not the breadth of the centre but its solidity, and that the advance of the centre pawns can often be deferred with advantage, provided always that care is taken to see that the opponent is not himself permitted to establish a strong centre.

Some of these points appear in the following examples. Let us make it clear, however, that even before 1914 there were some masters who did not accept the all-too-easy theories of the time; this goes without saying. Among them must be included Capablanca, Lasker, Nimzovitch and Rubinstein, though only Nimzovitch went so far as open criticism of the Tarrasch teachings.

First, some preliminary examples to illustrate what we mean by modern ideas. The game Bernstein–Nimzovitch, St. Petersburg,

1914, opened as follows: 1. P—Q4, Kt—KB3; 2. Kt—KB3, P—K3; 3. P—B4, P—QKt4; 4. Kt—B3, B—Kt2; 5. P—K3, B—Kt5. This must have seemed very odd at the time. After five moves Black still has no pawn in the centre and with 5. .... B—Kt5 he is deliberately preparing to exchange his K-Bishop (the attacking Bishop, as Tarrasch used to call it) for White's inoffensive Q-Knight. Nevertheless Black has freed his game. It all depends on the control of White's K4. Today the system is quite normal, under the name of Queen's Indian Defence.

The opening of the game Rubinstein–Alekhine, also from St. Petersburg, 1914, took the following course: 1. P—Q4, Kt—KB3; 2. P—QB4, P—K3; 3. Kt—QB3, B—Kt5; 4. P—K3, P—QKt3; 5. B—Q3, B—Kt2; 6. P—B3, P—B4; 7. P—QR3, B × Kt ch; 8. P × B, P—Q4. Tarrasch was completely at a loss to understand this opening, as is clear from his annotations in the tournament book. Of 2. .... P—K3 he remarked that this move can hardly have any other intention than to confuse White. He could not grasp the idea that Black was aiming to exert pressure against White's K4 in the quickest way—namely by means of B—QKt5 and B × Kt. On similar grounds he criticized 6. P—B3 and 8. .... P—Q4. Today's verdict is that both these players displayed fine feeling for the needs of the position. The opening is known today as one of the most important variations of one of the most played of all openings—the Nimzo-Indian Defence.

In a consultation game played in Zürich in 1921 Alekhine surprised his opponents, after 1. P—K4, with the reply 1. .... Kt—KB3. Can this be a good move? By the old criteria, certainly not, for by 2. P—K5, Kt—Q4; 3. P—QB4, Kt—Kt3; 4. P—Q4, P—Q3; 5. P—B4 White can form a massive centre—not to mention the old rule that a Knight on QKt3 is always badly placed. Yet nowadays the books give this as the main line of Alekhine's Defence. White's broad centre is too vulnerable to constitute an advantage.

The game Alekhine–Wolf, Pistyan, 1922, opened as follows: 1. P—Q4, P—Q4; 2. Kt—KB3, P—QB4; 3. P—B4, BP × P; 4. P × P, Kt—KB3; 5. Kt × P, P—QR3; 6. P—K4, Kt × KP; 7. Q—R4 ch, B—Q2; 8. Q—Kt3, Kt—B4; 9. Q—K3, P—KKt3; 10. Kt—KB3, Q—B2; 11. Q—B3, with an overwhelming game for White who, out of his eleven moves, has made four with the Queen, three with his K-Knight and four with pawns—dreadful play according to the old canons of economic development. But to the modern master no dictum was sacred.

The dominant characteristic of the inter-war modernism was independence of thought, especially as regards the interpretation and application of the rules of position play, and this automatically awakened a new enthusiasm for combination.

Attention must also be drawn to a sort of 'second edition' of supporters of the modern movement—a group of young men who achieved great things in the 1930s and very quickly attained almost complete hegemony in the chess world. One must say 'almost' for there were a few great players—with Alekhine first and foremost— who managed to withstand their onslaught.

These men worked along much the same lines as their immediate predecessors, but the broad principles had now been refined and perfected. We deal with Flohr, Fine, Reshevsky and Keres. Keres is a special case, standing at the meeting of two streams—where the play of the inter-war years mingles with that of the Russian school which is the subject of the next chapter. But it was in the western chess world that Keres received his first training and scored his first successes.

Now a few more worked-out examples:

GAME 31

Capablanca as forerunner of the modern masters. Here we see how Réti realized for the first time the difference between the dogmatic and the purposeful treatment of the pieces.

White: FÄHNDRICH & KAUFMANN   Black: CAPABLANCA & RÉTI
Consultation Game, Vienna, 1914.   *French Defence*

1. P—K4	P—K3	
2. P—Q4	P—Q4	
3. Kt—QB3	Kt—KB3	
4. P × P	P × P	
5. B—Q3	P—B4	
6. P × P	B × P	
7. B—KKt5	B—K3	
8. Kt—B3	Kt—B3	
9. 0—0	0—0	
10. Kt—K2	P—KR3	
11. B—R4	B—KKt5	
12. Kt—B3	Kt—Q5	
13. B—K2	Kt × B ch	
14. Q × Kt		

53

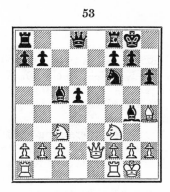

Here Réti commented as follows:

'A position was arrived at here in which the opportunity presented itself to develop a hitherto undeveloped piece and indeed with an attack. The move 14. .... R—K1 would have had that effect and was in accordance with the principles prevailing when I grew up and which corresponded almost entirely with Morphy's principles (for he would, without considering, have chosen that move). To my great astonishment Capablanca would not even consider the move at all. Finally he discovered the following manœuvre by means of which he forced a deterioration of White's pawn position and thereby later on his defeat.'

54

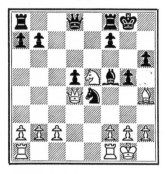

14.	....	B—Q5
15.	Q—Q3	B × QKt
16.	Q × B	Kt—K5
17.	Q—Q4	P—KKt4
18.	Kt—K5	B—B4

(See diagram 54)

19.	P—KB3	P × B
20.	P × Kt	B × P

White cannot extricate himself now by 21. Kt—Kt4 because of the reply 21. .... P—B4! After a tough struggle the Black allies succeeded in converting their advantage into a win as follows:
21. R—B2, P—R6; 22. R—K1, P—B4; 23. P × P, Q—B3; 24. Kt—B3, K—R2; 25. Q × Q, R × Q; 26. R—K3, R—QKt3; 27. P—Kt3, R—QB1; 28. Kt—Q4, R—KB3; 29. R—B4, K—Kt3; 30. P—B3, K—Kt4; 31. Kt—K2, R—R3; 32. P—R4 ch, K—B3; 33. P—R4, P—Kt4!; 34. P × P, R—R8 ch; 35. R—B1, R × R ch; 36. K × R, K—K4; 37. Kt—Q4, P—B5; 38. R—R3, R—KKt1; 39. K—K1, R—Kt8 ch; 40. K—K2, R—Kt7 ch; 41. K—B1, R—Kt7; 42. K—K1, P—KR4; 43. K—Q1, B—B4; 44. Kt × B, K × Kt; 45. P—B4, K—K5; 46. R—QB3, P—B6; 47. K—K1, P—Q5! White resigns.

A model of enterprising precision play in every phase of the game. 'With this game' said Réti, 'began a revolution in my conviction as to the wisdom of the old principle, according to which in the opening every move should develop another piece. I studied Capablanca's games and realized that contrary to all the masters of that period he had for some time ceased to adhere to that principle.'

Here, however, we must add that we do not unreservedly agree with Réti's judgment on this remarkable game, for it is not clear that the advantage obtained from the manœuvre 14. .... B—Q5 is absolutely forced.

Further investigation reveals that 19. P—KB3? was a weak move;

White should simply have played 19. B—Kt3! Against this Capablanca gave the following variation: 19. .... Kt × B; 20. BP × Kt, B × P; 21. Kt—Kt4, P—B4; 22. Kt—K3, B—K5; 23. QR—Q1, Q—Kt3; 24. Kt × QP, B × Kt; 25. Q × Q, P × Q; 26. R × B, R × P; and Black has won a pawn—which happens to be virtually worthless.

But White could have done better in this variation, and at two points. First, by 23. KR—Q1 instead of 23. QR—Q1 he could have won the Q-pawn without losing his own QR-pawn. Secondly 20. RP × Kt! would have been stronger than 20. BP × Kt. In that case White himself would have the advantage, for 20. .... B × P is now unfavourable because of 21. Kt—Kt4, P—B4; 22. Kt—K3, B—K5; 23. P—B3, P—B5; 24. P × P, etc., while other lines, e.g. 20. .... P—B3 instead of 20. .... B × P, would leave Black in some difficulties with his weakened pawn position.

Black has yet another attempt at his disposal. After 19. B—Kt3 he could try not 19. .... Kt × B but 19. .... P—KR4, threatening 20. .... P—R5. This looks very strong, but White has a nice continuation in 20. Kt—Q3, P—R5; 21. B—K5, P—B3; 22. B—B7!! and the Bishop escapes, for 22. .... Q × B; 23. Q × QP ch and 24. Q × B would cost Black a pawn.

This examination furnishes us with a different verdict on the critical manœuvre. Capablanca calls up some nice complications, but the conclusion that the 'modern' move 14. .... B—Q5 was stronger than the 'old-fashioned' one 14. .... R—K1—as Réti suggests—goes too far. It is however a good thing in itself to be able to confront the opponent with problems in any surprising way.

GAME 32

Richard Réti (1889–1929) was the great ringleader of the inter-war group of players. He had an extraordinarily sharp eye for what was happening on the board—not only in unusual situations but also in the commonplace ones. He created a variety of modern openings within the framework of the new thinking of the time. A very gifted strategist; not so talented as a tactician.

White: R. RÉTI   Black: T. GRUBER
Vienna, 1923.   *Réti System*

1. Kt—KB3

An old move, with a new intention. Zukertort used to open with this move, but he followed it up with 2. P—Q4. The Zukertort Opening was therefore no more than the Q-pawn Opening with transposition of moves. Réti however played 1. Kt—KB3 with the unusual aim of commanding two centre squares straight away (Q4 and especially

K5) without any rapid occupation of the centre with pawns. This aim cannot be attained by 1. Kt—QB3, or 1. P—KKt3, for Black would then play 1. .... P—K4, and easily obtain a satisfactory central formation.

1. ....   Kt—KB3

Black employs the same tactics. To 1. .... P—Q4 Réti used to reply not with Zukertort's 2. P—Q4 (occupation of the centre) but with 2. P—B4 (undermining of the opposing centre!).

2. P—B4

Now Black cannot very well play 2. .... P—K4 nor 2. .... P—Q4. The latter is not impossible, but by 3. P × P White would give himself the advantage of having two centre pawns to Black's one.

2. ....   P—Q3

Black must prepare to play P—K4 or P—Q4 as quickly as possible. Otherwise there is the danger of White suddenly throwing up his centre pawns with complete domination of the central zone.

The text move prepares P—K4; the safer alternative would be to prepare the central thrust P—Q4 by 2. .... P—B3 or 2. .... P—K3.

The symmetrical formation with 2. .... P—B4 is risky. With such a policy Black always runs the risk of suddenly having to abandon the symmetry in some disadvantageous way.

3. P—KKt3

Flank development of one Bishop—or both—is a natural

consequence of holding back the centre pawns.

3. ....   B—B4
4. B—Kt2   P—B3

Shortening the diagonal of the white Bishop and screening the black QKt-pawn in advance.

5. P—Kt3   Q—B1

A familiar manœuvre. Black intends 6. .... B—R6 forcing the exchange of the white K-Bishop and leaving White's 3. P—KKt3 as only a weakening of the K-side.

6. P—KR3

This parries the threat. True it leaves White unable to castle for some time but this is no hardship in a closed position.

6. ....   P—K4
7. B—Kt2   Kt—R3

Black avoids 7. .... QKt—Q2, which would give White a chance to castle.

8. Kt—B3   P—R3

This is an inconsequent move. Black prepares to withdraw his Bishop to R2, abandoning his original plan of preventing White from castling.

9. P—Q3   B—K2
10. Q—Q2   Kt—B2
11. Kt—Q1   0—0
12. Kt—K3   B—R2

See the previous note. The logical retreat was to K3. There is little point in Black's intended occupation of this square with a Knight.

13. 0—0

White takes the opportunity to castle.

13. ....   Kt—Q2

Preparing for P—KB4, but this move will bring no advantage.

14. Kt—R2!

White also prepares for P—KB4, and in this case it will achieve solid advantage, since it is combined with attack on the black centre. The encircling nature of the modern central strategy works out to perfection in this game. The two B-pawns carry out a pincer movement.

14. ....   Kt—K3
15. P—B4   P × P

This could have waited. Black should have chosen 15. .... P—KB4.

16. P × P

55

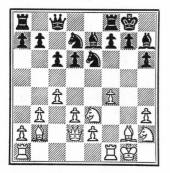

White was very well placed already, but Black's last move has given him three more important advantages: pawn majority in the centre; open diagonal QKt2—KKt7; open KKt-file.

Notice that the two white Bishops command all four centre squares. This is one of the advantages which flank strategy can bestow.

16. ....   P—KB4

Black cannot permit 17. P—B5.

17. K—R1   Kt—B3
18. R—KKt1!

White is not worried about losing the KB-pawn. The consequence of 18. .... Kt × P could be 19. Kt—Q5!, Kt(5) × Kt; (or 19. .... P × Kt; 20. Q × Kt, P × P; 21. B—Q5 ch, K—R1; 22. Q—Kt3, P—KKt4; 23. KtP × P, with overwhelming play for White); 20. P × Kt, P—B4 (of course not 20. .... Kt × P because of 21. B × Kt ch and 22. R × P ch); 21. B—KB3, K—R1 (22. Q × P was threatened); 22. R—Kt2, R—B2; 23. QR—KKt1, B—B1; 24. Kt—B1, followed by Kt—Kt3 and Kt—R5 with a winning attack.

18. ....   Kt—R4

Black threatens 19. .... Kt—Kt6 mate and at the same time puts another attack on the KB-pawn. Black probably hoped to capture the pawn under more favourable circumstances. The text move however augments the activity of the Q-Bishop.

19. B—KB3   Kt(4) × P
20. Kt—Q5!

The same pretty Knight move as in the above variation.

20. ....   Kt(5) × Kt

After this White wins by force. And if 20. .... P × Kt, White replies 21. P × P, regaining the piece with a fine attacking position.

21. P × Kt   B—Kt4

Black is lost. If 21. ....

P × P, White wins by 22. B × P, B—B3; 23. Q—K3, etc.

22. P × Kt!

Thus White wins a piece, for 22. .... B × Q fails against 23. R × P ch, K—R1; 24. R—Kt6 ch and mate in two. There followed:

22.	Q × P
23. Q—B3	B—B3
24. Q—Q2	K—R1
25. R—Kt2	R—B2
26. QR—KKt1	B—K4
27. P—Q4	B—B3
28. P—Q5	Resigns

GAME 33

Alexander Alekhine (1892–1946), the most important of all the players between the wars, reached the top by means of refined position play with strong attacking proclivities together with a rare talent for combination. Most of his combinations sprang from the soundly-based but dynamic build-up of his position. Alekhine has an impressive array of achievements to his name. He was moreover an outstanding authority on the openings—one of the few men of his day whose preparations did include study of the opening in depth. For a few years (1929–1934) during his tenure of the world championship his ascendancy over his nearest rivals was so great that whenever he took part in a tournament it was accepted in advance that he would inevitably take first prize.

The game about to be discussed was reckoned by Alekhine himself as one of the two best he ever played.

White: R. RÉTI   Black: A. ALEKHINE
Baden-Baden, 1925. *King's Fianchetto*

1. P—KKt3	P—K4
2. Kt—KB3	

Réti was addicted to opening experiments. His idea here is to play Alekhine's Defence (1. P—K4, Kt—KB3) with reversed colours and a move in hand. The extra move (P—KKt3), however, is more of a weakening than a reinforcement.

2.	P—K5
3. Kt—Q4	P—Q4

Unless he was absolutely sure of his ground Alekhine used to take great care to avoid any chance of his opponent taking the initiative in the opening. This explains why he rejected 3. ....

P—QB4; 4. Kt—Kt3, P—B5; 5. Kt—Q4, B—B4; the continuation which he afterwards indicated as favourable to Black.

4. P—Q3	P × P
5. Q × P	Kt—KB3
6. B—Kt2	B—Kt5 ch

Black wants to castle quickly. Subsequently he condemned this move on the grounds that the exchange of Bishops which follows leaves some slight weakness on the black squares in Black's position. The continuation of the game, however, does not seem to suggest that there is anything wrong with the move.

7. B—Q2

After 7. P—B3, B—K2 White would have lost a tempo, for his position requires an immediate P—QB4.

7.	B × B ch
8. Kt × B	O—O
9. P—QB4	

Preparing for Q-side operations. Exchange of the white QB-pawn for the black Q-pawn gives White the half-open QB-file and adds to the power of the fianchettoed Bishop.

9.	Kt—R3

Best. If 9. .... P—B4 the attacked Knight retires to QKt3 with an unpleasant double attack on Q5 and QB5.

10. P × P	Kt—Kt5
11. Q—B4	Kt(5) × QP
12. Kt(2)—Kt3	P—B3
13. O—O	R—K1
14. KR—Q1	B—Kt5
15. R—Q2	

What Black has in mind is B—R4—Kt3—K5; it follows that 15. P—KR3 would have been mere waste of time.

15.	Q—B1
16. Kt—QB5	

White has played logically and is now putting pressure on the black Q-side. The second part of his plan is the breakthrough by P—QKt4–5.

16.	B—R6!

From here on Black begins to work by combinative means. His aim, however, is only to maintain positional equilibrium. The text move offers a pawn which White cannot accept.

17. B—B3

Certainly not 17. B × B?, Q × B; 18. Kt × KtP? because of 18. .... Kt—KKt5; 19. Kt—B3, Kt(4)—K6!; 20. P × Kt, Kt × P; 21. Q × P ch, K—R1; 22. Kt—R4, R—KB1; mating or winning the Queen. A lovely combination!

17.	B—Kt5!
18. B—Kt2	B—R6!
19. B—B3	B—Kt5!
20. B—R1	

After some hesitation White resigns himself to this slightly inferior placing of his Bishop. He is playing for a win and so has practically no option.

20.	P—KR4!

Alekhine realizes that only by the most trenchant play will he be able to maintain equality. With this move he creates K-side attacking possibilities for himself.

21. P—Kt4	P—QR3
22. R—QB1	P—R5
23. P—R4	P × P
24. RP × P	

Black has weakened the white KKt-pawn and in what follows he profits from this one factor in grandiose fashion.

24.	Q—B2
25. P—Kt5?	

Consequent but not a good idea. White should have called off the attack on the Q-side in order to attend to his own safety. After 25. P—K4!, Kt—Kt3; 26. Q—Kt3, QKt—Q2 the chances would have been about equal.

25. ....   RP × P
26. P × P   R—K6!!

56

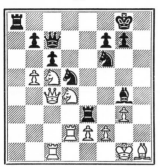

A pretty move, obvious enough in itself but extraordinarily deeply calculated. Black now threatens to win by 27. .... R × P ch; e.g. 28. P × R, Q × P ch; 29. B—Kt2, Kt—K6, etc.

27. Kt—B3?

This loses by force. White is indeed in trouble, yet still has chances of salvation according to Alekhine, who gave the following variations:

A. 27. K—R2?, R(1)—R6!
  (1) 28. P × R? Kt × P; followed by 29. .... Kt—B8 ch and Black wins.
  (2) 28. Kt(5)—Kt3, Q—K4; 29. P × P, P × P; and Black's attack is hardly to be withstood. If 30. P × R Black wins by 30. .... Q—R4 ch; 31. K—Kt1, Q—R6!

B. 27. B—B3!, B × B; 28. P × B, P × P; 29. Kt(4) × P, Q—R4! and Black, though very well placed, has not yet won. White cannot play 30. R × Kt? because of 30. .... R—K8 ch!; 31. R × R,

Q × R ch; 32. K—Kt2, R—R8! and Black wins.

27. ....   P × P
28. Q × P   Kt—B6!!
A sparkling new combination of rare depth.

29. Q × P
After 29. Q—B4, P—QKt4! Black wins much more easily.

29. ....   Q × Q
30. Kt × Q
Black's whole combination hinges on the unprotected position of this Knight.

30. ....   Kt × P ch
31. K—R2
Other moves are even less satisfactory: e.g.

A. 31. R × Kt. This Exchange sacrifice is hopeless; Black retains a winning attack.

B. 31. K—B1, Kt × P ch; 32. P × Kt, B × Kt; 33. B × B, R × B ch; 34. K—Kt2, R(1)—R6; 35. R—Q8 ch, K—R2; 36. R—R1 ch, K—Kt3; 37. R—R3, R(B)—QKt6! and Black wins. (Analysis by Alekhine.)

31. ....   Kt—K5!!
A brilliant continuation, and the only one which holds on to the advantage.

32. R—B4
The best chance. 32. P × R, Kt(5) × R loses the Exchange outright.

32. ....   Kt × BP!
At last Black wins a pawn and at the same time definitely removes the danger to his Rook.

But the combination has further to run yet.

It is worth noticing that any other move would have lost Black's advantage; e.g.

A. 32. .... Kt × R?; 33. Kt × Kt!, etc.

B. 32. .... R × Kt?; 33. R × Kt, etc.

33. B—Kt2   B—K3!

A very important part of the winning process. Black vacates his KKt5 for the Knight with gain of tempo. The rest now runs smoothly.

34. R(4)—B2   Kt—Kt5 ch
35. K—R3

This is forced and so are the rest of White's moves.

35.	Kt—K4 ch
36. K—R2	R × Kt
37. R × Kt	Kt—Kt5 ch
38. K—R3	Kt—K6 ch
39. K—R2	Kt × R
40. B × R	Kt—Q5

Now if 41. R—B2 there follows 41. .... Kt × B ch; 42. R × Kt, B—Q4! winning a piece. White is therefore bound to lose the Exchange and so resigns.

GAME 34

Aron Nimzovitch (1886–1935) is among the deepest chess thinkers of the 20th century. He established a few central themes and proceeded to build a whole theory upon them. They were, inter alia, the blockade, overprotection and pawn-chains. His practical abilities (as in the case of Réti) fell short of his theoretical accomplishments; nevertheless he belonged for many years to the little group of world-class players.

White: F. SÄMISCH   Black: A. NIMZOVITCH
Copenhagen, 1923.   *Queen's Indian Defence*

1. P—Q4	Kt—KB3
2. P—QB4	P—K3
3. Kt—KB3	P—QKt3
4. P—KKt3	B—Kt2
5. B—Kt2	B—K2
6. Kt—B3	0—0
7. 0—0	

All this is still usual today.

7. ....   P—Q4
7. .... Kt—K5 is also to be considered. White would continue 8. Q—B2.

8. Kt—K5   P—B3
9. P × P

Played presumably in the conviction that the simplification yields a slight advantage. This is not the case, and 9. P—Kt3 would therefore have been a little stronger.

9. ....   BP × P

It is true that the black Q-Bishop is now 'bad'; but the white K-Bishop, biting on the granite of Black's pawns on Q4 and K3, is not much better.

10. B—B4   P—QR3

The beginning of a process of constriction which continues right to the end of the game.

11. R—B1   P—QKt4

12. Q—Kt3
An idea worth consideration was 12. P—QR3, to hold up the advance of Black's QKt-pawn for the time being.

12. ....   Kt—B3!
Forcing the exchange of the active white Knight against the undeveloped black one.

13. Kt × Kt
Otherwise the black Knight goes via QR4 to QB5.

13. ....   B × Kt
14. P—KR3   Q—Q2!
By degrees the move P—Kt5 has become menacing and it cannot be prevented by 15. P—R3 for Black simply replies 15. .... P—QR4.

15. K—R2
White is unaware of the gathering storm and confines himself to consolidation.

15. ....   Kt—R4!
16. B—Q2   P—B4
17. Q—Q1   P—Kt5
At last comes this move—very unpleasant for White.

18. Kt—Kt1   B—QKt4
The bad Bishop comes into splendid action.

19. R—Kt1   B—Q3
20. P—K4?
Apparently very strong, for it threatens the black Knight. In fact, however, this move makes possible a positional combination which is rapidly decisive. 20. P—K3 was the correct move.

20. ....   BP × P!
21. Q × Kt   R × P

For the sacrificed piece Black has won two pawns but what is more important is the fact that he has substantially reinforced his scheme of encirclement. White can hardly lift a finger and his situation is going to get worse yet.

22. Q—Kt5
The Queen is not particularly well placed here but all other moves would have involved still greater difficulties.

22. ....   QR—KB1
23. K—R1
There was a threat of R(1)—B6, winning the KKt-pawn.

23. ....   R(1)—B4
24. Q—K3   B—Q6
25. QR—K1
Otherwise 25. .... R—K7 wins the white Queen.

25. ....   P—R3!!
The perfect blockade.

57

White resigns. He finds himself in absolute *zugzwang*. Apart from insignificant pawn moves like P—Kt3 and P—KR4, which can be met by a black King move, he has not a single move which does not lead to heavy material loss; e.g.

A. 26. K—R2, R(4)—B6 winning the white Queen.

B. 26. P—Kt4, R(4)—B6 again wins the Queen, for 27. B × R allows 27. .... R—R7 mate.

C. 26. B—QB1, B × Kt winning a Knight.

D. 26. R—QB1, R—K7 winning the Queen.

E. 26. B—KB1, B × B winning a piece.

Dr. Lasker hailed this game as the immortal *zugzwang* game.

GAME 35

Effim Bogolyubov (1889–1952), one of the strongest players of the 20th century, took the modern ideas of Réti and others and efficiently integrated them into his practical play. His play was sound and his style was primarily positional. In addition he had tactical talent which came into its own especially when the opponent had been outplayed strategically. His weak point lay in his optimism and lack of objectivity. 'When I am White I win because I am White; when I am Black I win because I am Bogolyubov.' It was because of this perhaps that Bogolyubov never quite scaled the topmost peak of the chess Olympus, though he came very near to it.

White: E. BOGOLYUBOV   Black: A. ALEKHINE

World Championship Match, 1929. The 18th Game. *French Defence*

1.	P—K4	P—K3
2.	P—Q4	P—Q4
3.	Kt—QB3	Kt—KB3
4.	B—Kt5	P × P

This variation was the centre of attention forty years ago and was generally considered satisfactory. Only later (and because of this game among others) did its drawbacks become evident.

5.	Kt × P	B—K2
6.	B × Kt	P × B

Here 6. .... B × B may be better; at least it is simpler.

7.	Kt—KB3	P—KB4

This immediate driving away of the Knight involves certain difficulties.

8.	Kt—B3	P—QB3

Black cannot allow White to play P—Q5 without a struggle.

9.	P—KKt3	Kt—Q2
10.	B—Kt2	Q—B2
11.	Q—K2	P—Kt4

Other moves would also have had their drawbacks; e.g. 11. .... Kt—B3; 12. 0—0—0, B—Q2; 13. B—R3 and now 13. .... 0—0—0 is impossible because of the reply 14. B × P. Or 11. .... P—Kt3; 12. 0—0—0, B—Kt2; 13. Kt—K5, R—KB1; 14. Q—B4. This last move is what the text move is intended to rule out. The double step of the QKt-pawn, though it introduces the possibility of P—Kt5, nevertheless amounts to a serious weakening.

12. Kt—K5!   B—Kt2

Not 12. .... Kt × Kt of course, because after 13. Q × Kt, Q × Q; 14. P × Q, Black cannot simultaneously parry 15. B × P and 15. Kt × P.

13. 0—0—0   Kt—Kt3
14. Q—R5   R—KB1
15. P—B4

White is in no hurry at all to capture the R-pawn, which will fall in due course like a ripe fruit. In any case the immediate capture would have been dangerous because of 15. .... B—B3 threatening to trap the Queen by 16. .... R—R1.

15. ....   P—Kt5
16. Kt—K2   Kt—Q4
17. B × Kt

An excellent appraisal of the situation. With this exchange White opens up the QB-file so that Black will be in considerable danger if he castles Q-side later on.

17. ....   BP × B
18. K—Kt1   P—R4

18. .... 0—0—0 would have been met by 19. P—B3 and 20. R—QB1.

19. P—Kt4!

Leaving the black position strategically bankrupt.

58

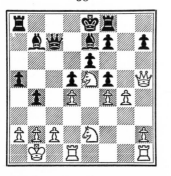

19. ....   P × P
20. P—B5!

The pretty positional sequel.

20. ....   P × P
21. Q × BP   P—R5
22. KR—K1

The results of White's break-through are now clear:

A. Pressure on the K-file, making the situation of the black King very unsafe.

B. Opportunity to bring the QKt into powerful play at KB4.

C. Alternative ways of recovering the sacrificed pawn.

22. ....   P—R6
23. P—Kt3   B—B1
24. Q × RP   B—K3

The K-file is now blocked but White has several more trumps in his hand.

25. Q—Q3   0—0—0

What else can he do?

26. P—B3!

Now the QB-file will play a very important part in the game.

26. ....   K—Kt2
27. R—QB1   Q—Kt3
28. P × P   B × P
29. R—B6!   Q—R4

After 29. .... B × R; 30. R × Q ch, K × R; 31. Kt—QB3, White wins just as quickly. (31. .... B × Kt; 32. Q × B, B—B4 ch; 33. K—R1, etc.)

30. R(1)—QB1   R—B1
31. Kt—KB4!

The black defences are cracking on all sides.

31. ....   B—Q3
32. Kt × B   P × Kt

33. Q—R7 ch	R—QB2
34. R × R ch	B × R
35. Q—Q7	Q—Kt3
36. Kt—Q3!	

The last decisive reserve joins in.

36.	R—Q1
37. R × B ch	

In such a position the combination will arise of its own accord.

37.	Q × R

38. Kt—B5 ch	K—Kt3
39. Q × Q ch	K × Q
40. Kt × P ch	K—Q2
41. Kt × R	K × Kt

Result of the combination: a sound extra pawn. It is enough. There followed 42. P—Kt4, K—Q2; 43. K—B2, K—B3; 44. K—Kt3, K—Kt4; 45. K × P, K—B5; 46. P—Kt5, K × KtP; 47. K—Kt3, K—R4; 48. P—QR4, K—R3; 49. K—Kt4, K—Kt3; 50. P—R5 ch, K—B3; 51. K—R4, and Black resigned.

Game 36

Salo Flohr (born 1908) represents the school of thought to which Fine and Reshevsky also belong. This group concerned itself mainly with positional finesses and microscopic details. Precise calculation of long sequences of moves played a large part in their style; unfathomable complications were avoided when possible. The consequence of these methods is that many of Flohr's games have a certain dryness about them. Against opponents of comparable strength he has played many draws, and has been justly dubbed 'The Drawing King'. Against slightly weaker opposition however Flohr is relentless.

White: S. FLOHR   Black: P. JOHNER

Berne, 1932.   *English Opening*

1. P—QB4	P—QB4
2. Kt—QB3	Kt—QB3
3. Kt—B3	P—KKt3
4. P—Q4	P × P
5. Kt × P	B—Kt2
6. Kt—B2	

An important move, making P—Q4 impossible for Black and keeping him cramped for a long time to come. There is also the point that after a later P—QKt3 by White there may be significance in the fact that the Q-Rook is protected by the Knight. The drawback to the move is the fact that Black can mutilate the white pawn position by exchanging on QB6. To do

so, however, would concede the two Bishops to White.

6.	P—Q3

All the same Black should have played 6. .... B × Kt ch. Now he comes under serious pressure.

7. Q—Q2

White prevents the pawn-doubling and prepares for the Q-fianchetto.

7.	Kt—B3
8. P—K4	

8. P—QKt3 would also have been possible, for the reply

8. .... Kt—K5 would cost a piece: 9. Kt × Kt, B × R; 10. Kt × B!

8.	P—QR3
9. B—K2	R—QKt1
10. 0—0	0—0
11. R—K1	B—Q2
12. R—Kt1	

White sets up a solid position and awaits the mistake which must soon occur.

| 12. .... | Q—B1 |
| 13. P—QKt3 | P—QKt4? |

This attempt to free the black game turns out badly. Black has looked five moves ahead; White has seen just a little further.

| 14. P × P | P × P |
| 15. B × P | Kt × P |

All according to plan.

| 16. R × Kt | B × Kt |
| 17. Q × B | R × B |

The end of Black's combination. Now for White's.

18. R—QB4!

59

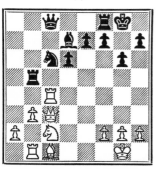

Notice that the obvious 18. B—R6 does not achieve anything because of 18. .... Kt—K4! (19. R—QB4, Q × R!). Now however 19. B—R6 is a powerful threat while 19. Kt—Q4 could also be a dangerous move.

18. ....   R—Q1?
Black's situation after 18. .... R—K1 would also have been unsatisfactory but in that case his game would still have been playable. Any attempt to force a quick win would have failed:

A. 19. Kt—Q4, Kt × Kt; 20. R × Q, Kt—K7 ch; 21. K—B1, Kt × Q; 22. R × Kt with equality.

B. 19. B—R6, P—K4; 20. Q—B3, Q—Q1! and White gets nowhere.

19. B—R6
The immediate 19. Kt—Q4 was also possible, but the move played is stronger.

19. ....   P—B3
Sad necessity. After 19. .... P—K4; 20. Q—B3, P—B4; White wins as follows: 21. Kt—R3! (but not 21. P—QR4?, Kt—Q5!; 22. Kt × Kt, Q × R!) 21. .... R—Kt3 (21. .... R—QR4; 22. P—QKt4!); 22. Q—Q5 ch, K—R1; 23. Q—B7.

20. Kt—Q4   R—Kt3
20. .... R—QB4 would have been better though still insufficient.

21. R—QB1
All calculated to a nicety.

| 21. .... | Kt × Kt |
| 22. R × Q | Kt—K7 ch |

23. K—B1	R × R
24. Q × R ch	B × Q
25. R × B ch	K—B2
26. B—K3!	

The finishing touch. Black is prevented from imprisoning the Bishop by 26. .... P—Kt4 and the black Knight is lost. Black resigns. All quite simple when once you see it.

GAME 37

Reuben Fine (born 1914) gave a combinative twist to Flohr's methods; consequently his games generally have a rather livelier character. His play is also marked by a great measure of adaptability and flexibility. Finally he has in his arsenal (as also has Reshevsky, his great compatriot and rival) the very important weapon of an all-but-infallible drawing technique. Whenever a half point is sufficient for his purposes, he can be 90 to 95 per cent. certain of getting it.

White: R. FINE   Black: A. ALEKHINE
Margate, 1937.   *Dutch Defence*

1. P—Q4	P—K3
2. P—QB4	P—KB4
3. P—KKt3	Kt—KB3
4. B—Kt2	B—Kt5 ch
5. B—Q2	B—K2

With this manœuvre Black argues that the white Bishop is less well placed at Q2 than at B1, since it cuts off the action of its own Queen on the Q-file.

6. Kt—QB3	Kt—B3

A defiant move, which allows White to assume a powerful initiative. 6. .... P—Q4 would have been safer and better.

7. P—Q5!	Kt—K4
8. Q—Kt3	0—0
9. Kt—R3	

In most variations of this opening this is the square for the K-Knight. The diagonal from KKt2 remains clear while the Knight often finds an active post at KB4.

9.	Kt—Kt3
10. P × P	

If White should permit 10. .... P—K4 and 11. .... P—Q3 Black would achieve a fine attacking position.

10.	P × P
11. R—Q1	

If 11. B × P the reply is not 11. .... R—Kt1 because of 12. B × B, R × Q; 13. B × P ch, K—R1; 14. P × R, and White has full value for the lost Queen. Black has a better line, however, in 11. .... B × B; 12. Q × B, R—Kt1; 13. Q × RP, R × P with promising counterplay.

11.	P—B3
12. 0—0	P—K4?

Black pushes on with his plans, but it soon becomes evident that Alekhine has overestimated his position. Either 12. .... K—R1 or 12. .... Q—B2 would have been better.

13. P—B5 ch

The ramifications of this move require precise calculation, for the advanced pawn is bound to be weak. But the Fine-Flohr school thrives on this sort of thing.

13. ....   K—R1
14. Kt—KKt5   Q—K1

Otherwise White wins the Exchange.

15. Kt—K6   B × Kt
16. Q × B   B × P

After 16. .... Q—B1; 17. Q × Q, QR × Q; 18. B—R3, Kt—Q2; 19. P—QKt4 White would have the advantage of the two Bishops—in the circumstances not an unimportant factor.

17. Q × KBP

From the point of view of material the games are level but positionally White is better off, his pawn position being far superior.

17. ....   R—Q1
18. Q—B2   Q—K3
19. Kt—R4   B—K2
20. P—QR3

Slowly but logically White now proceeds to make use of his advantage.

20. ....   R—Q5
21. P—R3

Not 21. Kt—B5? of course; Black would reply 21. .... B × Kt; 22. Q × B, R(1)—Q1, etc.

21. ....   P—Kt4

Forcing the Knight to return to B3, but also creating a Q-side weakness which will bring retribution later on.

22. Kt—B3   P—QR4
22. .... P—QR3, followed by

23. .... P—B4 was worth consideration.

23. B—K3   R × R
24. R × R   P—Kt5
25. P × P   P × P
26. Kt—R4

The only result of all Black's aggression is that his Q-side pawn position is now irremediably weakened.

26. ....   Kt—Q4
27. B—B5

Black now has—in effect—three isolated pawns.

27. ....   Q—B2

If Black exchanges at his QB4 he loses at least a pawn after the recapture 28. Q × B.

28. P—K3   R—B1
29. Q—B4!

60

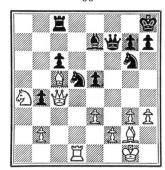

The first result of White's exact play: Black must lose a pawn.

29. ....   Q—B1

Otherwise White wins a piece by 30. P—K4.

30. B × B   Kt(3) × B

30. .... Q × B? would cost a piece (31. B × Kt).

31. P—K4	Kt—B3
32. Q × KtP	

White has not only won a pawn but has the better position into the bargain.

32.	R—Q1
33. R × R	Q × R
34. Kt—B5	Q—Q3
35. Q—B3	P—R3
36. Kt—Q3	

One of the characteristics of the style is an iron-strong endgame technique. There are very few of Fine's games in which an extra pawn is not converted into a win.

36.	Kt—Q2
37. P—R4	Kt—KKt3
38. B—R3	

All systematically done. The white Bishop is given a new line of action.

38.	Kt(3)—B1
39. P—QKt4	P—R4
40. Kt—B5	Kt—B3
41. Q—B4	Q—K2
42. Kt—Kt3	Q—Q3
43. Kt—R5	

The second pawn must fall.

43.	Q—Q7
44. Kt × P	Q—K8 ch
45. B—B1	Kt × P
46. Q—K2!	

Forcing off the Queens and settling the whole business. The rest of the game was:

46. .... Q × Q; 47. B × Q, P—Kt3; 48. Kt × P, Kt—B6; 49. B—Q3, K—Kt2; 50. P—B4, Kt—Q4; 51. P—Kt5, K—B3; 52. K—B2, Kt—Kt3; 53. K—K3, Kt—R5; 54. K—Q4, Kt—K3 ch; 55. K—Q5, Kt—B2 ch; 56. K—B6, Kt—K3; 57. P—Kt6, Kt—Q1 ch; 58. K—Q7, Kt—K3; 59. P—Kt7, Kt(5)—B4 ch; 60. K—B8 and Black resigned.

GAME 38

Samuel Reshevsky (born 1911) combined the qualities of Flohr and Fine, integrating them into one superb whole. His pertinacity in apparently barren positions was equalled only by his staying power and defensive skill under difficult and adverse conditions. Reshevsky has never propounded abstruse general theories; he is a pragmatist.

For many years he was in the running for the World Championship but the great Russian efflorescence which coincided exactly with his own best time prevented him from fulfilling this aspiration.

White: M. EUWE   Black: S. RESHEVSKY

Avro, 1938.   *King's Indian Defence*

1. P—Q4	Kt—KB3
2. P—QB4	P—KKt3
3. P—B3	P—Q4

The best line. Black accepts a minority in the centre in the interests of active piece-play.

4. P × P	Kt × P
5. P—K4	Kt—Kt3
6. Kt—B3	B—Kt2
7. B—K3	0—0
8. P—B4	

Although this move costs a

tempo it makes **KB3** available for a Knight as well as augmenting White's influence in the centre.

8. ....   Kt—B3!

Typical Reshevsky. He sacrifices two tempi in order to entice the white centre forward with the idea of attacking it later on.

9. P—Q5

If 9. Kt—B3 the reply 9. .... B—Kt5 is very strong.

9. ....   Kt—Kt1
10. Kt—B3

A sound enough move but 10. P—QR4 with P—R5 in view would have been stronger.

10. ....   P—QB3
11. Q—Kt3   P × P

After 11. .... B × Kt ch; 12. P × B, P × P; 13. B × Kt, P × B; 14. P × P, White would be very well placed.

12. Kt × P

More or less forced. After 12. P × P, B × Kt ch; 13. P × B, Q × P!; 14. B × Kt, Q—K5 ch! Black keeps the pawn.

12. ....   Kt × Kt
13. P × Kt   Kt—Q2
14. B—K2   Q—R4 ch

All played with precision. The obvious reply 15. K—B2 would now be met with 15. .... Kt—B3! with decisive advantage to Black.

15. B—Q2   Q—Kt3
16. B—B3   B × B ch
17. P × B   Q—K6!

White's insecure K-position is now giving him trouble.

18. P—B4

A pawn sacrifice which is just about forced. If 18. Q—B4 there follows 18. .... Kt—B3 with the unanswerable threat of 19. .... Kt—K5.

18. ....   Q × P
19. 0—0   Q—B2

Having secured his booty Reshevsky now prepares for careful defence.

20. K—R1   Kt—B3
21. Q—K3   B—Kt5
22. Q—R6

22. Kt—K5 was also to be considered here. The move played sets Black some nasty problems but it is in just such positions that Reshevsky is very much at home.

22. ......   B × Kt

The Knight must be eliminated, because of the threatened 23. Kt—Kt5 and 24. R × Kt.

23. R × B   P—QKt4!

61

This powerful positional counter-action is the point of Black's defence. White cannot now continue the attack with

24. R—KR3 because of 24. ....
Q—K4; 25. R—K1, P×P, etc.

24.	P×P	Q—K4
25.	R—K1	Kt×P
26.	R—R3	Q—Kt2
27.	Q—Q2	P—K3

White's attack is broken, but in view of the threatening attitude of the white Q-side pawns Black is still going to have trouble in converting his extra pawn into a win.

28.	R—Q3	QR—Kt1
29.	P—QR4	Kt—Kt3
30.	Q—Kt4	

Subsequent analysis revealed that 30. P—R5 would have been stronger: 30. .... Kt—B5; 31. Q—Kt4. Or 30. .... Kt—Q4; 31. R—QKt3.

30.	....	QR—B1
31.	P—R5	Kt—Q4
32.	Q—Kt3	R—B4

In time trouble (Reshevsky was always in time trouble; it was, in a manner of speaking, part and parcel of his play) Black here overlooks the still stronger move 32. .... Q—K4.

33.	B—B3	R—Kt1
34.	B×Kt	R(4)×P

35.	Q—R2	P×B
36.	R×P	Q—B6
37.	R—KB1	R—Kt7
38.	Q—R4	R—Kt8
39.	R(5)—Q1	

39. R(1)—Q1 would have been a little better. Then 39. ....
R×R ch; 40. Q×R.

39.	....	R×R
40.	R×R	P—QR3

The last move of the time pressure, and an uncommonly strong one. The white QR-pawn is fixed and from now on will be a weakness. Moreover 41. ....
R—Kt4 is prepared. There followed:

41. P—R3, R—Kt4; 42. R—R1, K—Kt2; 43. Q—R2, Q—Kt7; 44. Q—R4, R—Kt4; 45. R—KKt1, Q—B6; 46. R—R1, P—R4; 47. Q—R2, R—KB4; 48. K—R2, P—Kt4!; 49. Q—R4, R—B5; 50. Q—R2, P—Kt5; 51. P×P, Q—K4! (a pretty interpolation); 52. P—Kt3, R—K5; 53. Q—Kt1, R—K7 ch; 54. K—R3, P×P ch; 55. K—R4, R—R7 ch; 56. K×P, Q—K7 ch and White resigns. Reshevsky conducted the whole game—the endgame especially—with iron strength.

GAME 39

Paul Keres (born 1916) forms a link between the western Inter-War School and the eastern Soviet School. His play exhibits on the one hand the combinative richness of Alekhine, with a bias towards adventurousness, and on the other hand the solid positional basis of Smyslov and Petrosyan. A certain affinity is also discernible between the games of Keres and those of the venturesome Tal.

Since Keres is master of so many attacking weapons he is also well qualified to appraise the attacks of his opponents with great accuracy. He is thus a great attacker and also a great defender, and this combination of skills has brought him many successes.

Paul Keres has been at the pinnacle of international chess for more than thirty years but the goal of a match for the World Championship has always eluded him. In several eliminator series he has had to be content with second place. Hence his nickname, 'Paul the Second'.

White: P. KERES   Black: E. WALTHER

Tel Aviv Olympiad, 1964.   *King's Indian Defence*

1. P—Q4	Kt—KB3
2. P—QB4	P—KKt3
3. Kt—QB3	B—Kt2
4. P—K4	P—Q3
5. Kt—B3	0—0
6. B—K2	P—K4
7. P—Q5	

It is well known that White cannot play to win a pawn here: 7. P × P, P × P; 8. Q × Q, R × Q; 9. Kt × P, Kt × P! with advantage to Black.

7.	QKt—Q2
8. B—Kt5	

This prevents Black from quickly achieving P—KB4. There is no attacking significance in the move for White cannot reinforce the pin and also since Black can unpin at any moment.

8.	P—KR3
9. B—R4	P—KKt4

Another system is 9. .... P—R3 (to prevent Kt—QKt5) and then 10. .... Q—K1 and 11. .... Kt—R2. An objection to the text move is the weakening of the K-position.

10. B—Kt3	Kt—R4

Black presses on.

11. P—KR4!

Taken with what follows this is a deep plan. If White, relying on the hidden attack of his Bishop on K2 against the Knight, should try 11. Kt × KP or

11. Kt × KtP Black can interpolate 11. .... Kt × B; e.g. 11. Kt × KP, Kt × B; 12. Kt × Kt, Kt × B!; 13. Kt × R, Kt × Kt, etc.

11.	P—Kt5
12. Kt—R2	Kt × B

Forced, and apparently very strong.

13. P × Kt	P—KR4
14. 0—0	

Drawing up a balance we observe that the K-side is weakened for both players, but that both Kings are reasonably safe for the moment. Sooner or later however Black will have to play P—KB4 and then all the white pieces will spring directly into action.

14.	B—R3
15. B—Q3	P—QB3
16. K—R1	Kt—B3
17. B—B2	P × P
18. BP × P	Kt—K1
19. Q—K2	Kt—Kt2

Black now has everything in readiness for P—KB4, and White has also prepared all the necessary counter-measures.

20. R—B2	P—B4

If Black continues to refrain from this move White will get the advantage in the KB-file by such measures as Kt—KB1—K3 and then QR—KB1.

21. P × P   Kt × P
21. .... B × P would have
been less good because of
21. QR—KB1, Q—Q2; 23. B ×
B, and now:

A. 23. .... R × B; 24. Kt × P!,
P × Kt; 25. R × R, Kt × R;
26. Q × P ch, etc.

B. 23. .... Kt × B; 24. Q—
Q3, Kt—Kt2; 25. Kt—K4, etc.

22. B × Kt
After 22. Q—Q3, Q—K2;
23. QR—KB1 Black gets
counter-chances with 23. ....
P—K5! (24. Kt × KP, Q × Kt!).

22. ....   B × B
23. QR—KB1   B—Kt3
After 23. .... Q—Q2;
24. Kt—K4 White would be just
as favourably placed, but the
text move permits a continuation which is as surprising as it is
pretty.

24. Kt × P!

62

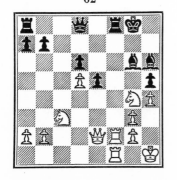

24. ....   P × Kt
25. Q × KtP   K—R2
If 25. .... Q—K1 White of
course plays 26. P—R5.

26. P—R5   B—Q6
27. R × R   B(3) × R
28. R—B3!
The obvious 28. R—B7 ch,
K—R1; 29. Kt—K4 would not
lead to any direct advantage
after 29. .... Q—B1! 30. Q—
Kt6, Q—B8 ch; 31. K—R2, Q—
R3.

28. ....   B—B7
But now the QB-file is blocked
and White can proceed with the
continuation given in the previous note.

29. R—B7 ch   K—R1
30. Kt—K4
Threatening 31. Q—Kt6 as
well as 31. Kt—B6.

30. ....   Q—K1
After 30. .... B × Kt; 31. Q ×
B, B—Kt2 there is the decisive
32. P—R6! And 30. .... Q—
B1 is useless of course, because
of 31. Q—Kt6, B × Kt; 32. R—
R7 mate.

31. Kt × P!
Another uncommonly powerful
move. After the obvious 31. Q—
Kt6 there follows 31. .... Q × R!;
32. Q × Q, B × Kt; and White is
faced with a long and dubious
endgame.

31. ....   Q—R5
If 31. .... Q—Q1 White wins
by 32. Kt—B5, Q—Kt3?; 33. R ×
B ch!

32. Q—Kt5
With new threats, the main
one being 33. P—R6 followed by
34. R × B ch or 34. Q—B6 ch.

32.	Q—R3
33. Q × P ch	

Or 33. R—Q7, which also wins.

33.	K—Kt1
34. R—B6	Q—Q6
35. K—R2	

Evading checks. It is note-

worthy how the King is permanently sheltered by his own doubled pawns.

35.	Q—R2
36. Q—K6 ch	

Black resigns. (36. .... K—R1; 37. Kt—B7 ch, K—Kt2; 38. P—R6 ch.)

NEW THIRST FOR BATTLE
The Russian School: 1945 to the Present Day

AFTER THE last World War a movement grew up in the Soviet Union to make chess a real game of the people. To achieve this goal the Russian players had to set about winning such renown that the government would be persuaded to grant chess a special position in the framework of Russian society.

This aim has been achieved in full; there is not the slightest doubt of that. The Russian chess federation numbers its members in millions. About half the holders of international titles live in Russia. The World Championship has been in Russian hands since 1948 and one gets the impression that it will stay there for some years yet. Famous names among the Russian stars include Botvinnik, Smyslov, Tal, Petrosyan (all holders of the World Championship at one time or another), Keres, Bronstein, Spassky, Geller, Taimanov, Kotov, Stein, Polugaievsky, Korchnoi and many others who have won and maintained the Russian hegemony in the chess world.

First priority with the Russians is the utilization of one's resources to the utmost; hence the following characteristics:

A. Struggle for the initiative.
B. Fighting spirit; no use for the formal draw.
C. Active defence, always on the lookout for a counter-thrust. It is remarkable how many fighting games are won by Black in Russia.
D. Careful study of the openings, especially combinative offshoots of disputed variations.
E. No superficial judgments on a position based on the measuring-rod of material. Which pieces are present matters less than what they can achieve.

One manifestation of all this is the so-called Russian Exchange. Very long-range sacrifices of the Exchange seem to occur more frequently in Russia than anywhere else.

To illustrate the style of the Russian School here are a few games by some of its leading representatives.

Mikhail Botvinnik (born 1911) who held the World Championship, with two short breaks, for fifteen years is one of the most typical members of the Russian School. His aim is always to seize the initiative. He is a remarkably deep combination player who can think out and compare long sequences of moves; but he is also an excellent position player, a good defender and a great master of the endgame. Remembering that Botvinnik is also very much at home in the domain of the openings, it is no exaggeration to say that Botvinnik is the most versatile champion in the history of chess. Only in excessively tedious and dull positions is he vulnerable and it was this one weakness which cost him the World Championship in his match with Petrosyan in 1963.

White: V. LYUBLINSKY　Black: M. BOTVINNIK
Moscow, 1943.　*Ruy Lopez*

1. P—K4	P—K4
2. Kt—KB3	Kt—QB3
3. B—Kt5	P—QR3
4. B—R4	Kt—B3
5. B × Kt	

There is a rather strange look about this exchange which looks like loss of time. The idea is quite simple. In the normal Lopez Exchange Variation (with B × Kt at move 4) Black protects his weak K-pawn by P—KB3. But after 4. .... Kt—B3 this simple protection is no longer available, and this fact may lead to various difficulties for Black.

5.	KtP × B

After 5. .... QP × B, which is reckoned stronger, White's objective comes out more clearly; e.g. 6. P—Q3, B—Q3 (guarding the K-pawn); 7. QKt—Q2, Kt—Q2; 8. Kt—B4 and Black's position is slightly inferior.

6. Kt—B3	

Theory prefers 6. P—Q4 or 6. Kt × P.

6.	P—Q3

7. P—Q4	Kt—Q2

This move is often played in such positions though in playing it Black accepts a serious weakening of his Q-side.

7. .... P × P; 8. Kt × P, B—Q2 deserved consideration. (9. Q—B3, P—B4; 10. Kt—B5, B × Kt; Alekhine–Capablanca, St. Petersburg, 1914.)

8. P × P	P × P
9. 0—0	B—Q3
10. Kt—K2	0—0
11. Kt—Kt3	R—Kt1
12. P—Kt3	R—K1
13. B—K3	P—Kt3
14. P—B3	P—QR4
15. Q—B2	Q—K2
16. KR—Q1	Kt—B4

Although Black's position on the Q-side leaves something to be desired this does not prevent him from playing for the initiative by hook or by crook. The fact that this strategy may sooner or later lead to less favourable positions does not worry Black. This is the essential characteristic of a game keenly conducted on both sides.

17. Kt—K1	Kt—K3
18. Kt—Q3	Kt—B5
19. P—B3	B—R3

This forces White to a weakening move, from which Black hopes shortly to profit.

20. P—B4	P—QB4

More or less forced but it does look as though Black has not achieved anything. White's P—QB4 weakened his Q4 square, but Black's P—QB4 weakened the pawn itself. The latter seems the more serious.

21. Q—Q2!	

Simultaneously attacking KB4 and QR5. Black's reply is therefore forced.

21.	Kt × Kt
22. Q × Kt	KR—Q1
23. Kt—K2	P—QB3

This prevents the Knight from penetrating to Q5.

24. Kt—B3	B—B2
25. Q—B2	R—Q5!

The Russian Exchange sacrifice. Should White accept it Black will have a protected passed pawn; even more important is the fact that the black pieces will have an enhanced freedom of movement while White's will find themselves very much tied down.

26. Kt—K2?	

A faulty appraisal. White decides that it will be better to part with his Knight rather than his Bishop in exchange for the intruding Rook, but the reverse is true. In these half-closed positions the Knight is generally stronger than the Bishop. By 26. B × R, BP × B; 27. Kt—R4

followed by 28. Kt—Kt2 the white Knight could be brought to the blockade square Q3, from where it would develop great activity.

26.	B—B1
27. Kt × R	BP × Kt
28. B—B2	

White should have brought the Bishop to Q2 in order to prepare the counter-thrust P—QKt4 as quickly as possible.

28.	P—QB4
29. R—KB1	P—B4
30. B—Kt3	

White remains passive on the Q-side which is exactly where his chances lie.

30.	B—Q2
31. QR—K1	P—B5
32. B—B2	P—Kt4!
33. P—KKt4?	

Again, mistaken strategy. This move seriously weakens the white K-position.

33.	P × P e.p.
34. B × KtP	B—R6

The Bishop had certainly never dreamed of reaching such a powerful position as this.

35. R—B2	P—R4!
36. R—Q2	P—KR5
37. B—B2	R—KB1!

Introducing the decisive attack. It is very clear that in this position neither of the white Rooks is as strong as the black Bishop on R6. White's win of the Exchange therefore counts for absolutely nothing.

38. R—Q3	R—B5
39. K—R1	K—R2
40. R—KKt1	B—Q1

Freeing the Queen from her task of guarding the Kt-pawn.

| 41. Q—K2 | Q—KB2 |
| 42. Q—Q1 | Q—R4 |

After an immediate 42. .... P—Kt5 there follows 43. P × P, R × B; 44. R × B, and Black's attack is not yet decisive. After the text move, however, Black does threaten 43. .... P—Kt5 with dire consequences.

63

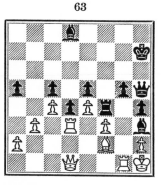

Should White now continue with 43. B—K1 the decisive sequel would be 43. .... P—

Kt5; 44. P × P, B × P; 45. R × B (forced); 45. .... Q × R; 46. Q × Q, R × Q; and Black wins the K-pawn, after which his pair of united passed pawns, with Bishops on the same colour, give him an easy win.

43. B—K3

White seeks salvation in Bishops on opposite colours—the drawing device par excellence.

43.	Q × P ch
44. Q × Q	R × Q
45. B × KtP	R × R
46. B × B	R—K6

The combination is over. Black gets his pair of united passed pawns which, notwithstanding the presence of Bishops on opposite colours, will easily win the game. The finish was:

47. B—Kt6, R × KP; 48. B × BP, R—K7; 49. R—Q1, B—Kt5; 50. P—KR3, B × P; 51. P—Kt4, B—B4; 52. B—Q6, P—Q6; 53. P × P, P—R6.

White resigns.

*Vassily Smyslov (born 1921) took over the World Championship in
1957 and held it for one year. He has emulated Botvinnik with great
tournament and match successes.*

*His style, though just as typically Russian, contrasts strongly with
that of Botvinnik. Smyslov builds his game mainly on a positional
basis—though this is by no means to say that he fights shy of combination.
The general aspect of his style is pacific but the methods he uses to attain
his goal are not always what they seem. He is less direct but stealthy,
and all the more dangerous for that.*

*Smyslov is also an outstanding master of the openings, as becomes clear
in the following game.*

White: V. SMYSLOV   Black: S. RESHEVSKY

U.S.S.R. v. U.S.A., Radio Match, 1945. *Ruy Lopez*

1.	P—K4	P—K4
2.	Kt—KB3	Kt—QB3
3.	B—Kt5	P—QR3
4.	B—R4	Kt—B3
5.	0—0	Kt × P

The so-called Open Variation
of the Lopez. 5. .... B—K2
is the Closed Variation.

6.	P—Q4	P—QKt4
7.	B—Kt3	P—Q4
8.	P × P	B—K3
9.	P—B3	B—QB4

9. .... B—K2 is more usual
today.

10.	QKt—Q2	0—0
11.	B—B2	P—B4
12.	Kt—Kt3	B—Kt3
13.	KKt—Q4	Kt × Kt
14.	Kt × Kt	B × Kt
15.	P × B	P—B5

Leading to one of the most
hotly disputed variations of the
open Ruy Lopez. Black intends
to sacrifice a piece.

16.	P—B3	Kt—Kt6
17.	P × Kt	P × P
18.	Q—Q3!	

Typically Russian. White pro-
poses to return the extra material
at once in the interests of improving his position. The idea is
18. .... Q—R5; 19. Q × RP ch,
Q × Q; 20. B × Q ch, K × B;
21. B—Q2, with an ending in
White's favour.

18.	....	B—B4
19.	Q × B	R × Q
20.	B × R	Q—R5
21.	B—R3	Q × P ch
22.	K—R1	Q × KP

64

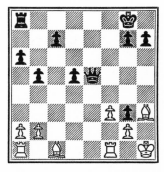

We are now at the critical
position of what the books have

come to call, for obvious reasons, 'The Long Variation'.

23. B—Q2!   Q × P?
Too greedy. Black hastens to secure united passed pawns but these would have materialized in due course. He should have chosen 23. .... P—B4. Now he loses the important advanced pawn.

24. B—B4   P—B4
There would have been better defensive possibilities in 24. .... P—Q5.

25. B—K6 ch   K—R1
26. B × QP
Now that the fate of Black's pawn on Kt6 is sealed it is safe for the white K-Bishop to break contact with the defence square KR3.

26. ....   R—Q1
27. QR—Q1   P—B5
28. B × KtP   P—B6

Not 28. .... Q × RP because of 29. B × P!

29. B—K5
White lines up his Bishops for the decisive mating attack.

29. ....   P—Kt5
30. B—QKt3   R—Q7
31. P—B4   P—KR4
32. R—QKt1   R—KB7(!)
33. KR—K1!   Q—Q7
34. QR—Q1   Q—Kt7
35. R—Q8 ch
It is all over. Reshevsky has been American champion for many years, and he excels above all in defence—but not even he can hold out against the hurricane which now breaks:

35. .... K—R2; 36. B—Kt8 ch, K—Kt3; 37. R—Q6 ch, K—B4; 38. B—K6 ch, K—Kt3; 39. B—Q5 ch, K—R2; 40. B—K4 ch, K—Kt1; 41. B—Kt6!
    Black resigns.

GAME 42

Mikhail Tal (born 1936) like Smyslov was World Champion for a short time. His style displays all the typically Russian characteristics, and in extreme form.

Tal is a cavalier without fear or reproach. In powers of combination he perhaps outdoes even Alekhine. Sacrifice is second nature to him. Whereas most masters will make a sacrifice only when, by study of its variations, they have convinced themselves of its soundness, Tal is prepared to make any sacrifice unless he can definitely demonstrate it to be unsound.

To stand up to Tal one must first of all be a very fine defender; secondly, to be able to keep one's head in face of Tal's dynamic and often bizarre methods, one needs nerves of iron.

White: M. TAL   Black: B. LARSEN

Candidates' match, 1965.   10th and last game. *Sicilian Defence*

1. P—K4	P—QB4
2. Kt—KB3	Kt—QB3
3. P—Q4	P × P
4. Kt × P	P—K3
5. Kt—QB3	P—Q3
6. B—K3	

White means to castle quickly on the Q-side, hoping to create attacking chances.

6.	Kt—B3
7. P—B4	B—K2
8. Q—B3	0—0
9. 0—0—0	

An enterprising set-up—castling on opposite wings. White is all ready for an attack on the K-side while Black must seek his fortune on the other flank.

9.	Q—B2

Black would have liked to play 9. .... P—QR3 to prevent the Knight-incursion which follows. This move, however, would have allowed White to break through immediately in the centre: 9. .... P—QR3?; 10. P—K5!, P × P?; 11. Kt × Kt.

10. Kt(4)—Kt5	Q—Kt1
11. P—KKt4	

Tal in his element.

11.	P—QR3
12. Kt—Q4	Kt × Kt
13. B × Kt	P—QKt4

An obvious move here would be 13. .... P—K4; but it would not lead to an advantage for Black. There would follow 14. P—Kt5, B—Kt5; 15. Q—Kt3, B × R; 16. P × Kt, B × KBP; 17. Kt—Q5! The continuation could now be:

A. 17. .... P × B; 18. Kt × B ch, K—R1; 19. R—Kt1, etc.

B. 17. .... Q—Q1; 18. B—Kt6, P × P; 19. Q—Kt1, etc.

C. 17. .... B—Q1; 18. P × P, B—KR4; 19. P—K6, B—KKt3; 20. P—K7, etc.

Another possibility (after 13. .... P—K4) is 14. P—Kt5!, B—Kt5; 15. Q—Kt3, P × B!; 16. P × Kt, P × Kt; 17. P × B, P × P ch; 18. K—Kt1, B × R; 19. R—Kt1, P—KKt3; 20. P ×

R(Q) ch, Q × Q; 21. B—B4, B—R4; 22. B—Q5, leaving White with the better chances.

14. P—Kt5	Kt—Q2
15. B—Q3	P—Kt5
16. Kt—Q5!!	

65

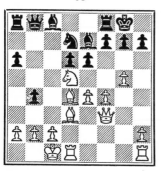

The critical position of the game, and a situation typical of Tal's methods. The sacrifice is not correct, but neither is it incorrect. For the sacrificed Knight White will have one pawn and several valuable lines of attack. The defender's task will be arduous but perhaps not impossible.

| 16. .... | P × Kt |
| 17. P × P | |

Threatening not only the obvious 18. Q—K4 but also the familiar double Bishop sacrifice 18. B × P ch, K × B; 19. Q—R5 ch, K—Kt1; 20. B × P!, K × B; 21. Q—R6 ch, K—Kt1; 22. P—Kt6 and wins. However, Black can easily defend himself.

| 17. .... | P—B4 |
| 18. QR—K1 | R—B2 |

After 18. .... B—Q1 White's attack proceeds with 19. Q—R5. e.g. 19. .... Kt—B4; 20. B × KtP!, Kt × B ch; 21. K—Kt1! and now:

A. 21. .... K × B; 22. Q—R6 ch, K—Kt1; 23. P—Kt6, Q—B2; 24. QR—Kt1, etc.

B. 21. .... Kt × R; 22. P—Kt6!, K × B; 23. Q × P ch, K—B3; 24. P—Kt7, etc. (24. .... R—B2?; 25. P—Kt8(Kt) mate).

| 19. P—KR4 | B—Kt2 |

19. .... Kt—B4 would have made it less easy for White to develop the full power of his attack; e.g. 20. P—R5, Kt × B ch; 21. Q × Kt, B—B1; 22. P—Kt6, R—K2; 23. P × P ch, K × P; 24. R × R, B × R; 25. Q—KKt3.

| 20. B × BP | |

Tal himself suggested the strong alternative 20. P—Kt6, P × P; 21. P—R5, P—Kt4; 22. B × BP., e.g. 22. .... R × B; 23. R × B, Kt—K4; 24. P—R6! Or 22. .... Kt—B1; 23. P—R6, P—Kt3; 24. P—R7 ch, etc.

| 20. .... | R × B |

After 20. .... Kt—B1; 21. P—R5 the white attack is also very strong; e.g. 21. .... Q—Q1; 22. B × P ch, Kt × B; 23. P—Kt6, R × P (apparently the refutation, for 24. Q × R would be met by 24. .... B—Kt4); 24. R × B! and wins.

| 21. R × B | Kt—K4 |

Another difficult point in this exciting game. If 20. .... R—B2, which seems to bring White's efforts to a dead end, there follows 22. R × R, K × R; 23. P—Kt6 ch!, P × P; 24. P—R5! and the attack is still rolling. After the move actually played White regains his sacrificed material.

22. Q—K4   Q—KB1
22. .... R—B2 would be clearly refuted by 23. R × R, Kt × R; 24. P—Kt6.

23. P × Kt   R—B5
24. Q—K3
The white Queen must continue to attack Black's hanging Rook; otherwise Black could safely capture on his K2.

24. ....   R—B6?
After 24. .... B × P the result would still have been an open question, though the line 25. P × P, R × R; 26. Q × R, B × R; 27. Q × QKtP would certainly have left White with the better chances.

25. Q—K2   Q × R
26. Q × R   P × P
27. R—K1   R—Q1
28. R × P   Q—Q3
29. Q—B4!
Indirectly protecting the Q-pawn, for 29. .... B × P loses to 30. R—K8 ch! White now has two sound extra pawns and wins with ease. The finish was:

29. .... R—KB1; 30. Q—K4, P—Kt6 (an attempt to sow confusion); 31. RP × P, R—B8 ch; 32. K—Q2, Q—Kt5 ch; 33. P—B3, Q—Q3; 34. B—B5! (By his very nature Tal must always find a sacrifice. There is not the slightest doubt about the soundness of this one.) 34. .... Q × B; 35. R—K8 ch, R—B1; 36. Q—K6 ch, K—R1; 37. Q—B7!
Black resigns.

GAME 43

Tigran Petrosyan (born 1929) convincingly defeated Botvinnik to win the World Championship in 1963. He is one of the most accomplished strategists in the history of chess, but in contrast to his colleagues he scores most of his positional victories not by intuition but by precise calculation.

He is at home in all sorts of positions. He can conduct an attack with élan and has registered many successes by mating attacks after the Queens have gone. Equally Petrosyan is a past master of defence, which he manages in active style in accordance with the principles of his national school.

Petrosyan prefers to avoid risks and consequently is seldom beaten. On the other hand his percentage of draws is substantially higher than that of most Soviet players.

White: T. Petrosyan   Black: Kozali

Montevideo, 1954.   *Queen's Gambit, Exchange Variation*

1. P—Q4   Kt—KB3
2. P—QB4   P—K3
3. Kt—QB3   P—Q4
4. P × P

The Exchange Variation is today regarded as one of the most powerful weapons of the Q-Gambit. The Russian players in particular have a liking for this line and not because they are looking for quick simplification. The simplification, for that matter, is only apparent; the Exchange Variation leads as a rule to a sharp struggle, either on the Q-side or in the centre.

4. ....   P × P
5. B—Kt5   QKt—Q2
6. P—K3

6. Kt × P? is a well-known little joke: 6. .... Kt × Kt; 7. B × Q, B—Kt5 ch and Black wins.

6. ....   B—K2
7. B—Q3   0—0
8. KKt—K2

White chooses the most effective set-up. The white KKt is better placed at K2 than at KB3, especially in view of a later Kt—K5 by Black.

8. ....   R—K1
9. Q—B2   P—B3
10. P—KR3

Always a useful move in this variation. It has two points: it deprives the black pieces of the use of their KKt5 and at the same time provides the white Q-Bishop with a possible retreat square on KR2.

10. ....   Kt—K5
11. B—KB4!

Exchange of pieces would favour the defender.

11. ....   Kt(2)—B3
12. P—B3   Kt × Kt
13. P × Kt   B—Q3
14. B × B   Q × B
15. P—K4!

This powerful central advance is a direct outcome of White's chosen Exchange Variation.

15. ....   Kt—R4
15. .... Kt—Q2 would have been more prudent, but Black is out for counter-attack.

16. P—K5   Q—R3
The KR-pawn must be protected.

17. Q—Q2!!

66

The White King is not particularly safe in the centre; moreover both flanks contain weaknesses which render them unattractive as shelters for the King. Exchange of Queens would therefore suit White. But the text move is more than a safety precaution: it is the best preparation for the intensive prosecution of an attack against the black King.

17. ....   Q × Q ch
Black cannot avoid the Queen exchange for 17. .... Q—K3 would cost a piece after 18. P—Kt4.

18. K × Q   P—KKt3
19. P—Kt4   Kt—Kt2
20. P—KR4   P—KR3
Quite correctly Black tries to keep the K-side closed. 21. P—

R5 would now be met by
21. .... P—KKt4.

21. QR—KB1
With this move and his next
White prepares the advance of
his KB-pawn.

21.	B—Q2
22. KR—Kt1	P—QKt4
23. P—KB4!	P—QR4

Black looks for salvation on
the other wing. He cannot hold
back the white K-side advance.

24. P—B5!
With the deadly threat of
25. P—K6, BP × P; 26. P—B6,
winning the Knight.

(See diagram 67)

| 24. .... | P × P |

Practically forced; but now
the storm really breaks.

| 25. P × P | K—R1 |
| 26. P—K6! | |

67

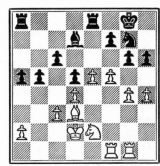

Position after White's 24th move

A sharply calculated finish.

| 26. .... | P × P |
| 27. P—B6 | Kt—B4 |

If 27. .... Kt—R4 the Knight
is lost after 28. B—Kt6.

| 28. B × Kt | P × B |
| 29. R—Kt7!! | |

Black resigns. After 29. ....
KR—Q1; 30. Kt—B4, B—K1;
31. R(1)—KKt1 Black's only
choice is between mate or loss of
a piece.

Boris Spassky (born 1937) obtained the grandmaster title at the age of eighteen but it took several more years for his powers to develop to the full. His greatest successes came in 1965 when in set matches he defeated Keres, Geller and Tal in succession. In the following year he won the Piatigorsky Tournament at Santa Monica in front of Fischer, Larsen, Petrosyan, Reshevsky and other grandmasters.

Spassky has no single strongly-pronounced style; his games show contrasting methods. He can be enterprising but also cautious; he can be liberal with his pieces but also thrifty; he can play by intuition but also by accurate calculation; but at all times he is ready for a fight, and this makes him a worthy representative of the Russian School of Chess.

White: P. KERES   Black: B. SPASSKY

Candidates Match, Riga, 1965.   10th and last game.

King's Indian Defence, Four Pawns Variation

1. P—Q4	Kt—KB3
2. P—QB4	P—KKt3
3. Kt—QB3	B—Kt2
4. P—K4	P—Q3
5. P—B4	

An enterprising build-up, with many incisive lines.

5.	P—B4

Following the general principle that a broad centre must be assailed without delay.

6. P—Q5	0—0
7. Kt—B3	P—K3

The same idea: weakening the enemy centre.

8. B—K2	P × P
9. BP × P	

The usual move is KP × P, giving White some small territorial advantage. The move played tries for more—perhaps for too much. White maintains his central majority but his K-pawn is vulnerable. The result of this strategy is that if White is to turn his majority to account

he will have to push on still further in the centre with unforeseeable consequences.

9.	P—QKt4

An indirect attack on the white centre. He is threatening 10. .... P—Kt5, and intends to meet 10. B × P with 10. .... Kt × KP! Then 11. Kt × Kt, Q—R4 ch; 12. Q—Q2, Q × B; 13. Kt × QP, Q—R3; 14. Kt × B, R—K1 ch; 15. K—B2, Kt—Q2; and Black has enough compensation for the sacrificial material. A striking example of the undermining of a broad centre.

10. P—K5

To a certain extent this is forced, but in any case it is a very promising move.

10.	P × P
11. P × P	Kt—Kt5

The position is difficult to assess; the white pawns seem weak and yet strong. White's trouble is that his development is so backward.

12. B—KB4

This is stronger than 12. B—Kt5, which would lead to very good play for Black: 12. .... P—B3; 13. P×P, B×P; 14. B×B, Q×B; 15. Kt×P, B—Q2!, etc.

12. .... Kt—Q2

Forcing the advance which follows.

13. P—K6 P×P

13. .... Kt—K4 was also worth considering, but Black is not afraid of the coming complications.

14. P×P R×B
15. Q—Q5

68

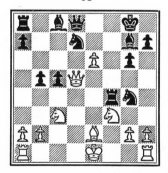

A position loaded with dynamite. White has three threats: 16. P—K7 ch, 16. P×Kt ch and 16. Q×R.

15. .... K—R1
16. Q×R

White has won the Exchange but the black pieces are well posted and White has still to castle.

16. .... Kt—Kt3
17. Q×P

After 17. Q—Kt8 Black continues very strongly with 17. .... Kt—K6! protecting the Rook indirectly (18. Q×R?, Kt×P ch). Another possibility was 17. Q—B6 but it is doubtful if it would have been any better than the move played.

17. .... B×P

White is the clear Exchange ahead, but who can deny that in the circumstances either of the black Bishops is at least as strong as one of the white Rooks? This is a typical demonstration of the 'Russian Exchange'.

18. 0—0 Kt—K6
19. R—B2

The return of the Exchange by 19. QR—Q1 came in for consideration here, but Black would have retained enough advantage; e.g. 19. .... Kt×QR; 20. R×Kt, B—Q5 ch; 21. K—R1, P—Kt5; 22. Kt—QKt5, B—Q4! (23. QKt×B, P×Kt; 24. Kt×P, R×Kt; 25. R×R, B×P ch; 26. K×B, Q×R.)

19. .... P—Kt5
20. Kt—QKt5

The white pieces are scattered and open to attack. The attempt to consolidate by 20. Kt—Q1 would leave Black with a strong attack after 20. .... Kt—Kt5; 21. R—KB1, B—Q5 ch; 22. K—R1, Q—Q3; 23. P—KKt3, B—Q4.

20. .... R—B2
21. Q—R5 Q—QKt1

Threatening 22. .... Kt—Kt5.

22. R—K1
Meaning to answer 22. ....
Kt—Kt5 with 23. B—B1.

22.	B—Q4
23. B—B1	

69

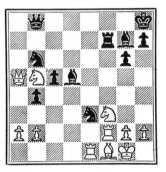

The alternative 23. B—Q3 would also give Black some difficulties. Bondarevsky gave the following variations: 23. B—Q3, Kt(3)—B5;

A. 24. Q—R6, Kt × KKtP; 25. K × Kt, Q—B5; 26. R—K8 ch, B—B1.
In this position Black's attack would probably carry most weight.

B. 24. B × Kt, Kt × B; 25. Q—R6, R—B3; 26. Q—R4, and now not 26. .... B—B3? because of 27. Q—R7, Q × Kt; 28. R—K7, but 26. .... R—B1 with the double threat of 27. .... B—B3 and 27. .... Kt × P.

23.	Kt × B
24. R(2) × Kt	Kt—B5
25. Q—R6	R—B3
26. Q—R4	Kt × P

26. .... B—B3 would again have been answered by 27. Q—R7! (27. .... Q × Kt; 28. R—K7).

27. Q—B2?
White could still have held out by 27. Q—R5, e.g. 27. .... Kt—B5?; 28. Q—B7!, Q × Kt; 29. Q—Q8 ch, B—Kt1; 30. R—K8. Black however has the better line 27. .... Kt—Q6, maintaining a certain advantage.

27.	Q × Kt

White cannot now play 28. Q × Kt because of 28. .... R × Kt. He is therefore left with a Rook against two Bishops, with no compensation. The finish was:

28. R—K7, Kt—Q6; 29. Q—K2, P—B5; 30. R—K8 ch, R—B1; 31. R × R ch, B × R; 32. Kt—Kt5, B—B4 ch; 33. K—R1, Q—Q2; 34. Q—Q2, Q—K2; 35. Kt—B3, Q—K6.
White resigns.